TRUSTEES & THE FUTURE OF FOUNDATIONS

JOHN W. NASON

Foreword by Robert F. Goheen

**COUNCIL
ON
FOUNDATIONS
New York**

Foreword

TRUSTEES AND DIRECTORS of all sorts of private institutions have been learning that many Americans no longer accept as given the utility, efficiency, or even the legitimacy of self-perpetuating boards. Foundations have not escaped this questioning and skepticism. They are challenged to confront in useful ways the problems of a complex and shifting society, and increasingly the spotlight comes to rest on the responsibilities and performance of their trustees. In this context neither the recommendations of the Filer Commission calling for greater diversity and accessibility on the part of foundation boards nor the more stringent proposals of the Donee Group, seeking to enforce such changes by law, are sports; they are instead symptomatic.

Well in advance of the findings of those two groups, toward the close of 1974, the directors of the Council on Foundations had concluded that a thorough, dispassionate study of foundation trustees and trusteeship should be mounted in order both to illuminate public understanding and to offer guidance to foundation trustees. At that same time, Dr. John W. Nason was nearing the end of his fine, searching, and persuasive study of college and university trusteeship conducted under the auspices of the Association of Governing Boards. That study was published in April 1975 under the title *The Future of Trusteeship: the Role and Responsibilities of College and University Boards.*

John Nason appeared to us then, as he has proved to be in fact, uniquely qualified to carry out the independent, knowledgeable inquiry that we sought. Formerly president of Swarthmore and Carleton Colleges, he is chairman of the board of the Edward W. Hazen Foundation. In addition he was for eight years a trustee of The Danforth Foundation and for three years served as chairman of the Advisory Committee of the Exxon Education Foundation. But above all John Nason respects facts and has no hesitation about presenting them as they are, without subterfuge or apology, as he makes his own reasoned judgments.

We are most grateful to him for agreeing to undertake this study, as we are also to the eleven foundations which provided the funding for it — namely, the Carnegie Corporation of New York, Cummins Engine Foundation, Exxon Education Foundation, Maurice Falk Medical Fund, General Service Foundation, Paul and Mary Haas Foundation, Charles F. Kettering Foundation, Lilly Endowment, Inc., New York Community

Trust, Rockefeller Brothers Fund, and Russell Sage Foundation.

Recognition is also due to the members of the Advisory Panel who have provided invaluable comment and criticism as Dr. Nason has worked through the successive stages of investigating and writing. Chosen to be representative of various foundation sizes and types and also to include "consumers" and other external interests, the membership of the Advisory Panel was: **Luis Alvarez,** National Urban Fellows; **Elmer L. Andersen,** The Bush Foundation; **Robert G. Chollar,** Charles F. Kettering Foundation; **Anita Straub Darrow,** Wieboldt Foundation; **Pablo Eisenberg,** Center for Community Change; **Martha W. Griffiths,** Griffiths & Griffiths, Farmington Hills, Michigan; **Watts Hill, Jr.,** financial and higher educational consultant, Chapel Hill, North Carolina, and trustee, Southern Education Foundation; **M. Carl Holman,** President, Urban Coalition; **Mrs. Drue King, Jr.,** President, Cleveland YWCA and member, Distribution Committee, The Cleveland Foundation; **Leslie L. Luttgens,** Rosenberg Foundation; **Maryanne Mott Meynet,** The Charles Stewart Mott Foundation; **William Parsons,** Milbank, Tweed, Hadley & McCloy, New York City and Chairman, Distribution Committee, New York Community Trust; **Henry E. Russell,** President, Boston Safe Deposit and Trust Company; **Alexander B. Trowbridge, Jr.,** Vice Chairman, Allied Chemical Corp., Morristown, New Jersey, and trustee, Hattie M. Strong Foundation and Frank E. Gannett Newspaper Foundation; **Paul N. Ylvisaker,** Dean, Graduate School of Education, Harvard University, and trustee, Mary Reynolds Babcock Foundation and Dayton Hudson Foundation.

From the start it was agreed that this was to be John Nason's study and report. Neither the Council's Board, which has followed his work with interest, nor the Advisory Panel, which has contributed much through consultation, can claim editorial responsibility. He was asked to make his own investigation and develop a report that would express his own findings and convictions. This precisely is what John Nason has done.

In my opinion he has done it superbly well. Foundation trustees and others concerned about the role of foundations in today's world will find much here to inform and to light the way forward toward responsible and telling foundation performance.

Robert F. Goheen

Mr. Goheen, President of The Edna McConnell Clark Foundation, was Chairman of the Council on Foundations, October 1972-January 1977.

Preface

THE EGALITARIAN TEMPER of the present time has encouraged a critical examination of established institutions and of the traditional claims to authority of those who control those institutions. The directors of business corporations are facing new challenges and in response are accepting new responsibilities. The trustees of colleges and universities, the directors of hospitals and museums, indeed all those in authority are struggling with new problems and new ways of dealing with them.

Foundation trustees are no exception. In fact, since foundation trustees, more than in most types of institutions, are the foundation, and since foundations occupy a relatively privileged position among American institutions, it was inevitable that the nature, attitudes and performance of their trustees would come in for close scrutiny. Sporadic attacks from quite divergent points of view during the first six decades of the century were succeeded during the 1960s by Representative Patman's persistent campaign. That campaign resulted in the Tax Reform Act of 1969 which, for all its punitive aspects, reaffirmed once again the legitimate and important role of private philanthropy, including the foundations, in American life. Populist aversion to large concentrations of wealth and to its control by private groups, however, is endemic in the American democratic tradition. The relative calm of the 1970s provides, therefore, an opportune time to take a fresh look at the role and responsibilities of foundation trustees and to prepare for the next round of attacks.

Much is known about the trustees of the largest foundations, but that knowledge becomes thin as one works one's way down through the pyramid of foundations where the great bulk of trustees live and move and have their being. Some members of the Advisory Panel felt that the time had come for a complete census of the 100,000 or more foundation trustees, or at least a set of reasonably accurate profiles based on a scientific sampling of the entire group. Somewhat reluctantly we decided against this. Professional advice on the size of the sample and the techniques for obtaining and tabulating replies indicated that the cost in time and money would be prohibitive.

The procedure finally adopted was to interview trustees and staff members across the country. Anxious to avoid an Eastern seaboard emphasis, I traveled to the South, the Midwest, Texas, and the West coast from Los Angeles to Seattle in addition to the major East coast cities. So far as possible I talked with trustees of all kinds of foundations, though the quite small family foundations were under-represented in my sampling. Altogether I talked with just under 200 individuals from 157 foundations, of which 70 were private foundations with assets of $10 million or more, 65 private foundations with assets of under $10 million, 12 community foundations and 10 company-sponsored foundations. These interviews were supplemented by participation in regional and national meetings of trustees where foundation problems were discussed, by two specially convened meetings of trustees, one in Minneapolis and the other in Atlanta, to review my findings and tentative conclusions, and by periodic meetings of the Advisory Panel.

The impressions I brought back from the interviews were very mixed. I found many statesmen of the first order, fully aware of the dangers and of the responsibilities, men and women of vision, sensitivity and courage. But in other quarters I found a high degree of complacency and privacy. Many trustees see no clouds on the horizon now that the Tax Reform Act of 1969 has eliminated "abuses" and satisfied the critics. Many are too preoccupied with day-to-day decisions even to think about future problems. Most trustees will admit, when pressed, that the funds they control are no longer strictly private money but money committed to the service of the public good. For many, however, this is a nominal admission, an abstract proposition not always reflected in their actions. They continue to think of the foundation as the donor's, or as "ours," and resent suggestions for greater accountability, greater accessibility, greater diversity of viewpoints on the board. While regional and local associations of foundations are growing, large numbers of trustees still shy away from any form of cooperation. There lingers an aura of privacy about the foundation world as well as a reluctance to recognize changes in society requiring different standards of performance.

It is not hard to understand why this is so. There was a time when foundations were largely thought of as extensions of individual giving. To many a donor the foundation was the equivalent of another bank account on which he could draw for charitable contributions. And just as he was unwilling to brook interference from outsiders, whether the government or groups within the community, in giving away his personal funds, so he was unwilling to allow interference in the affairs of his foundation. Times have changed, and the values by which we judge institutions today are different from those used earlier in the century. Fifty years ago no one judged a corporation evil because it dumped its wastes into public streams. Today we think differently, and foundations are being judged by today's standards and expectations.

The research on which this study is based, while building on the labors of experienced scholars such as F. Emerson Andrews, dean of all "foundation watchers," does not produce the kind of hard data on which an objective analysis of all foundation trustees might be based. Indeed, there is a personal and even impressionistic character to the record of my interviews, for I often found that what was not said, or the way in which it was said, was as revealing of trustee attitudes and convictions as the actual words themselves. I found individuals who represented the highest quality of responsible trusteeship. I found others who had given little or no thought to their responsibilities or who, while talking a good game, performed poorly.

There were more of the latter than I had anticipated, which suggests that it is time for foundation trustees to take a fresh look at themselves and their performance. I present in this report the conclusions and recommendations to which eighteen months of travel and study have led me. I do so with the hope that they may encourage all trustees to think more seriously about their crucial role in the preservation of an important American institution. Foundations have too important a contribution to make to American society to let them go by default.

The form and character of this study owe much to the members of the Advisory Panel whose counsel—collective, individual and occasionally conflicting—has helped me to see the problems of trusteeship in clearer perspective. I am indebted to the officers of the Council who never wearied of providing information when needed and of answering my innumerable questions. Both Robert F. Goheen, chairman of the Council during most of the course of this study and now president of The Edna McConnell Clark Foundation, and David F. Freeman, president of the Council, have been patient and encouraging throughout my uprisings and downsittings, reading the manuscript with critical eyes and saving me from many an error. Without the expert and indefatigable assistance of Sally Miller Watson, research assistant at the Council, this study would never have been completed; and in its final stages Marilyn Bradley proved indispensable. I am grateful, finally, to the 200 trustees and staff members who gave so generously of their time and revealed so candidly their insights, attitudes and convictions. Since our conversations were off the record, I have refrained from identifying sources, but much of the pith and substance of this study stem from them.

J.W.N.

Keene, N.Y.
February 1977

Contents

1   The Foundation Universe

"The Ford Foundation . . . is a large body of money completely surrounded by people who want some."

DWIGHT MACDONALD*

"One clear sign of the lack of public understanding of foundations is the widespread belief that there is a monolithic sameness to them, when, in fact, few types of organizations are as varied as they are in every respect."

PETERSON COMMISSION REPORT

THIS IS AN examination of the role and responsibilities of the considerable number of men and women who serve as foundation trustees. While in no sense a comprehensive study of foundations themselves, it nevertheless offers an assessment of their present status, since trustee attitudes and actions make foundations what they are. "A foundation," writes Robert K. Greenleaf, "is essentially a group of trustees who manage a pool of uncommitted funds that can be used for a wide range of socially useful purposes. This is a very privileged role, not just for what can be accomplished by giving money, but for the opportunity for the foundation to make itself a model of institutional quality, integrity and effectiveness."[1] Before plunging into an analysis of the problems and responsibilities which trustees carry, it may be helpful to make a brief survey of the foundation universe.

According to Edition 5 (1975) of *The Foundation Directory* there are 26,000 philanthropic foundations in the United States. The Foundation Center has data on 25,000, based for the most part on 1972 and 1973 reports. Their total assets are in the neighborhood of $31.5 billion, and according to the 1976 Annual Report of the American Association of

---

*The quotation sources of this and succeeding chapters may be found on pages 107-8.

1. "The Trustee: The Buck Starts Here" in *Foundation News,* July/August, 1973, p. 31.

Fund-Raising Counsel they made grants of $2.01 billion, or 7.5% of private charitable giving in 1975.[2]

The following table gives a breakdown by size:

Asset Size	Number of Foundations
Under $1 million	22,421
$1 -$5 million	1,699
$5 -$10 million	356
$10-$25 million	265
$25-$100 million	146
$100 million and up	38
	24,925

In the last category three—Ford, Lilly and Robert Wood Johnson—have assets in excess of $1 billion. In the group with under $1 million in assets 18,349, or 82%, have assets under $200,000; 15,580, or 69%, have assets under $100,000. The 22,421 foundations with assets under $1 million constitute 90% of the foundation universe and make grants totaling 20% of all foundation giving.

For the purposes of this study a foundation may be defined as "a nongovernmental, nonprofit organization with funds and program managed by its own trustees or directors, and established to maintain or aid social, educational, charitable, religious or other activities serving the common welfare, primarily through the making of grants."[3] Foundations may be classified in several ways—by size, purpose, source of funds, type of control, location. Some are operating foundations, i.e., foundations which use their funds primarily for their own programs and make few grants to other organizations unless in furtherance of their

---

2. For perspective compare these figures with those of some leading American corporations:

	Assets
Am. Tel. and Tel.	$74 billion
BankAmerica Corp.	60 billion
Prudential Life	39 billion
Exxon	31 billion

Exxon's 1975 profits of $3.1 billion were 50% higher than all foundation grants. IBM's net income of $1.8 billion was 85% of all foundation grants.

3. *The Foundation Directory,* Edition 5, Columbia University Press, 1975, p. xi. Discussions of the taxonomy of foundations will be found in the Introduction to *The Foundation Directory;* F. Emerson Andrews' classic work, *Philanthropic Foundations,* Russell Sage Foundation, 1956, chapter 1; *Philanthropic Foundations in the United States,* a brochure published in 1969 by The Foundation Center; *Foundations, Private Giving, and Public Policy,* the Report and Recommendations of the Commission on Foundations and Private Philanthropy (hereafter referred to as the Peterson Report), University of Chicago Press, 1970, chapter 5; *Revised Report and Recommendations to the Commission on Private Philanthropy and Public Needs on Private Philanthropic Foundations* by the chairman and staff of the Council on Foundations, August 1975, chapter II. For a brief and clear account of the many and complex statutory distinctions among the various categories of foundations and between private foundations and public charities, see the paper written by Laurens Williams and Donald V. Moorehead, "An Analysis of the Federal Tax Distinctions between Public and Private Charitable Organizations," November 1974, as a background study for the Commission on Private Philanthropy and Public Needs (the Filer Commission).

own programs. The great majority, however, are grant-making foundations. In recent years a number of governmentally financed organizations, such as the National Science Foundation and the National Endowment for the Arts, have been created. They fall outside the scope of this study which is concerned with private foundations and community foundations.

The private foundation world is usually divided into five groups or types. (1) *General purpose* foundations have the broadest mandate—to promote in one way or another the welfare of mankind. Most of the large foundations belong here. They are less likely to be family controlled and for the most part are managed by competent professional staff. They provide slightly over half of all foundation grants. (2) *Special purpose* foundations may be either large or small. By the donor's mandate or by subsequent decision of the trustees the foundation concentrates on limited objectives, such as cancer research, scholarship programs, the welfare of a social group or geographical community. (3) *Family* foundations constitute the largest group. Established for the most part by gifts from living donors, they are normally treated as vehicles for continuing the personal philanthropy of the donor. Donald R. Young, former president of the Russell Sage Foundation, characterizes them as "proprietary" foundations which "essentially are instruments of personal convenience for the donor, his family, and possibly his heirs."[4] Their capital assets are usually small, and they account for approximately 20% of all foundation giving. Some family foundations have very distinguished records. Many of the large general purpose foundations have evolved out of small family foundation beginnings. "Their designation here as proprietary is by no means intended as a disparagement," writes Young, "but only to suggest that they should be recognized as what they are in fact."

(4) A fourth class consists of *company-sponsored* foundations. Largely the result of post-World War II business growth they serve chiefly as conduits for corporate philanthropy, though some company foundations have accumulated substantial capital assets. While over 50% of corporate philanthropy is made directly by the parent company rather than channeled through a foundation, the latter has the great merit of compensating for fluctuations in the profit picture and permitting a steady flow of grants. Corporate giving tends to be viewed by company officers and directors as an aspect of public relations with grants to scholarship programs for employee children and to hospitals, recreational facilities and United Ways in communities where large numbers of employees live. Some company-sponsored foundations, however, have developed quite sophisticated programs of giving. The Dayton Hudson Foundation, Sears-Roebuck Foundation, Exxon Education Foundation, to name only three, are among the leaders. There are approximately 1,500 company-sponsored foundations.

(5) The 220 *community* foundations in the United States are a uniquely

---

4. Donald R. Young and Wilbert E. Moore, *Trusteeship and the Management of Foundations,* Russell Sage Foundation, 1969, p. 149.

3

favored species of the genus foundation under current tax law. The foundations composing the first four groups are classified by the Internal Revenue Service as private foundations. As such they are subject to certain restrictions and requirements of the Tax Reform Act of 1969. Community foundations, however, are collections of separate funds and trusts, some of which are designated for specific organizations. Their assets are normally managed by one or more trust companies, and the distribution of grants is made by a board of directors for those organized as corporations and by a distribution committee for those organized as trusts. Since they receive their funds from multiple sources, they are considered by IRS to be "public charities" along with 240,000 other 501(c)(3) agencies and institutions. Nevertheless, they are grant-making institutions with an honorable ancestry and substantial assets. The Cleveland Foundation goes back to 1914. The New York Community Trust has assets of just under $200 million and each year makes grants adding up to $10 million.

One further distinction is worth mentioning. There is a group (the exact number is unknown) of grant-making foundations classified under highly technical provisions of the 1969 Tax Reform Act as "supporting organizations." Exempt, like community foundations, from most of the restrictions imposed by the Tax Reform Act on private foundations, they make grants in support of a limited number (carefully specified) of educational and charitable organizations.

Who are the people who run these foundations and how many of them are there? Carl A. Gerstacker, trustee of the Gerstacker and Pardee Foundations, estimates between 140,000 and 150,000. A more conservative estimate would place them between 100,000 and 130,000. No one, however, has taken a complete census.[5] Nor do we know as much as we would like about the people who control foundations. From various analyses of selected groups of foundations we know that trustees are predominantly male, Protestant, university educated, well to do, and in their late fifties or early sixties. They are drawn chiefly from the legal and business worlds with a fair sprinkling of educators. Recent studies indicate an increase in women members to 19% and some slight increase in minority group members, but the latter still represent only 0.3%. We shall have more to say about the composition of foundation boards in chapter 6.

For the moment it is sufficient to point out that the number of trustees is significantly large and that, for understandable if not entirely defensible reasons, they tend to represent the Establishment and its values. Their actual responsibilities will vary with the nature of the foundation of which they are trustees. It is hardly reasonable to expect all trustees to give the time, energy and thought required of the trustees

---

5. For Gerstacker's estimates see his article, "Let 'Outsiders' Control Family Foundation Boards," in *Foundation News*, September/October, 1975. Gerstacker used Edition 5 of *The Foundation Directory.* If one were to use Edition 4 which lists 5,454 foundations and 23,000 trustees, or 4.2 trustees per foundation, the total for 26,000 foundations would be 109,200. Both calculations should be reduced by some arbitrary amount, say 10%, to allow for fewer trustees on the boards of the smaller unlisted foundations.

of The Ford Foundation who control the largest single source of private philanthropy in the Western world. The trustees of small family foundations, closer in most cases to both the donor and to the recipients, can afford to be more personal in their giving. Trustees of general purpose foundations face different problems from those of special purpose foundations. But intelligent, responsible trusteeship is required of all. The trustee who dispenses $10,000 a year has no more right to ignore his moral and legal responsibilities than the trustee who approves grants of $100,000,000.

2   Trustees: Private Almoners or Public Servants?

> "Foundation funds ... offer a case where a technically private asset is of such potential value to the nation that it must, perforce, be regarded as a public asset. The implications of this proposition are far reaching."
>
> ALAN PIFER

CENTRAL TO ANY understanding of the role of foundation trustees is the issue: are they spending or giving away strictly private money or money which can and should be considered as in some sense public? Are foundations merely a systematic way of carrying on the personal charitable interests of the donor or donors? Or does the public, whose interests are presumably being served by foundation grants, have some sort of vested interest in how the money is spent? To whom are trustees primarily responsible—to the donor or to the beneficiaries? It begs the issue to answer uncritically "to both." It might be closer to the mark to say "to neither." The primary responsibility of trustees is to maintain those standards of performance which are the inherent imperatives of trusteeship and which have evolved over centuries as embodying what is right, just and in the public interest.

It is easy to follow the reasoning of those who emphasize the private character of foundations. People of wealth, having made or inherited their money, are free to spend it as they wish, subject to payment of taxes and avoidance of illegal activities. Theirs is the choice to devote it to houses and horses, to the support of relatives and friends, to making more money, to the welfare of mankind. Most people do not question their right to give to college A rather than to university B, to religion rather than to art museums, to organizations bolstering the status quo rather than to those seeking some change in our society. Why, then, should anyone seek to limit the exercise of their private preference if and when they elect to systematize their philanthropy through the establishment of foundations? Have not they and their trustee successors the same unfettered right to direct foundation expenditures to whatever institutions and causes they personally prefer?

Foundation assets, however, are funds which have been legally committed to serving public purposes. Government funds also exist for that purpose. It is, however, a logical fallacy to argue, as some advocates do, that foundation money is basically government money, which the government allows private individuals to hold, invest and dispense. Until such a connection is established, we are justified in treating foundation funds as private assets, but let us be clear that they are not the property of any individual or group of individuals. "The important principle to be borne in mind at all times is that the foundation is a fiduciary for the public. Its property is dedicated to the service of the public and may not be used for private purposes or private profit. The creators of the foundation have no further rights in the property after they have dedicated it to the service of the public."[1]

A foundation is a charitable trust, and the trustees of such charitable trusts, whether they are in the form of corporate foundations or living or testamentary trusts, are *fiduciaries*. As such they have a double responsibility: to carry out the terms of the charter (presumably the intent of the donor) and to look after the interests of the beneficiaries. Trustees are held accountable by law for both. This applies not only to private trusts where the beneficiary is an individual and where no tax exemption is applicable, but also to charitable trusts which are not taxable because they serve the public welfare. Foundation trustees are servants of the public because the public, whether in broad or limited aspects, are the beneficiaries.

It is perhaps worth noting that the trustees of foundations and other charitable trusts are apt to be faced with a different mix of problems from those with which the trustees of private trusts must deal. Trustees of foundations have two distinct functions: the investment and management of the assets and the distribution or expenditure of available funds to appropriate recipients or programs. In carrying out the first of these functions, foundation trustees must act in a similar manner to trustees of private trusts. They must invest the funds with a view to the preservation of the corpus (even with an eye on growth in these inflationary times) and with a view to the production of income to be paid out to beneficiaries or expended on programs in the public interest. Along with the trustees of private trusts, they must follow a prudent course of investment, avoid conflicts of interest, and assume full responsibility for whatever actions have been delegated.[2] In fulfilling the second set of functions, however, their role is normally quite different. Occasionally the trustees of private trusts (e.g., in so-called sprinkle

1. Carl S. Stern, attorney and vice president of the Fred L. Lavenburg Foundation, *Proceedings of the Sixth Biennial Conference on Charitable Foundations*, New York University, 1963, pp. 8-9. Stern adds in a footnote: "Even on dissolution, no private person, no descendant or heir of the founder, for example, has any right to receive any part of the properties. It must continue to be devoted to the public service."

2. These are discussed in detail in chapter 11.

trusts) must select the beneficiaries from a designated group, whereas the selection of such beneficiaries is a major responsibility of foundation trustees. This is also a fiduciary function, but it requires an entirely different kind of expertise.

There are those, as noted earlier in this chapter, who argue that foundation money is really the government's money. If it had not been set up in a tax exempt foundation, a substantial portion of it—as much as 70% in fact—would have found its way into government coffers through the application of income or estate and inheritance taxes. One vigorous exponent of this view is Professor Stanley S. Surrey of the Harvard Law School and former Assistant Secretary of the Treasury for Tax Policy, who applies the same logic to all charitable deductions and to certain other forms of tax abatement. Since the government has the right to tax all income, and indeed all assets—so runs this theory—the loss of government income due to various tax exemptions and deductions is equivalent to an expenditure of government funds. Surrey was responsible for establishing in 1968 a "tax expenditure budget" for the federal government, so that the total federal budget might reflect both direct expenditures and income not received because of special tax arrangements. The practice has been continued in the intervening years.

The thrust of this argument is that the sum of $26 billion of private philanthropy in 1975, or at least a substantial portion of it, is really government money which the government allows private individuals and agencies to spend on its behalf. This seems tailor-made for those who object to the present system of tax deductions. It certainly provides powerful ammunition for those who would prefer that the government have complete control over all expenditures for the public welfare.

There are, however, both theoretical and practical difficulties with the concept of tax exemption as a form of tax expenditure. Its premise is the proposition that taxation is an inherent right of government rather than a power conferred on government by decision of the people governed. It took a Constitutional Amendment to give the federal government the authority to tax individual and corporate income, and even this authority was not extended to cover such institutions as churches and schools which serve the public interest. For a variety of practical reasons the Congress has from time to time expanded or contracted the charitable deduction; but that does not change the fact that exemption from taxation, while it may be limited by government, is not an act of grace on the government's part, but a recognition of a right not to be taxed except as the result of specific popular action.[3]

Furthermore, if exemptions from any given rate structure are tax expenditures, and if the government has the inherent right to set the rate structure at any level, all income between the highest rate and 100% is in theory an exemption and therefore a tax expenditure. This is

3. See the exchange of arguments between Professors Surrey and Hellmuth on the one side and Professor Boris I. Bittker of the Yale Law School on the other in Professor Bittker's "A Reply to Professors Surrey and Hellmuth" in the *National Tax Journal*, 1969, vol. 22, no. 539, pp. 538-42; and also Bittker's "Charitable Contributions: Tax Deductions or Matching Grants?" in the *Tax Law Review*, 1972, vol. 28, pp. 37-63.

patently absurd, and the scholastic subtleties of those who follow this line of reasoning will be persuasive only to those who are already convinced that all contributions to the public good should be channeled through government. What is at stake is a broad issue of public policy. The United States has a long and honorable history of private initiative on behalf of the general public. Do we wish to abandon this and settle for centralized government control of all aspects of welfare, or do we want to continue the freedom and diversity of multiple sources of funds and of decisions, both public and private?

Professor Milton Katz of the Harvard Law School sums up the counter-argument well in an essay he wrote nearly ten years ago:

> "The process of taxation converts private income into governmental funds. By no means does it follow that untaxed income may be regarded as 'government money' released to the original donor. It would require a 'Through the Looking Glass' logic to achieve such a metamorphosis.... Untaxed income covers all income that is not taxed, whether it simply falls outside the scope of an applicable revenue act or is specifically 'excluded' from a statutory definition of 'taxable income' or is declared by the statute to be 'exempt' or 'deductible.' The nub of the business is a decision to tax or not to tax.... The decision reflects a legislative judgment of policy. In the case of philanthropic donations the decision not to tax gives effect to a policy of fostering multiple and diversified bases for the financial support of education, research, health services, welfare, and community cultural services in the United States."[4]

A popular and less sophisticated variation of the view that foundation money is government money masquerading in private garb results from the belief that charitable contributions in general and gifts establishing foundations in particular are tax breaks or dodges or loopholes. Lumped together with other devices used to minimize taxes—investment in non-taxable securities, oil depletion allowances, artificially developed business losses and other kinds of tax shelters—they look to the uncritical like one more way by which the wealthy save money.[5] Unlike most loopholes, however, which are designed to save the taxpayer money, charitable contributions cost the individual money. The donor gives more than he would otherwise pay in taxes. The fact that the net tax cost to a donor in the 70% bracket of a gift of $100,000 is only $30,000 does not alter the fact that he is out $100,000. Benevolence has cost him more than using the money for his personal satisfactions; and while the U.S.

---

4. *The Modern Foundation: Its Dual Character, Public and Private*, Occasional Papers: Number Two, published by the Foundation Library Center, 1968, p. 14. The Report of the Filer Commission, *Giving in America*, contains a thoughtful analysis of these issues. See especially chapters I and V. See also an excellent brief account by Robert F. Goheen, chairman of the Council on Foundations, in the *Ripon Forum* for February 1974, entitled "Is Private Philanthropy 'Government Money'?"

5. See, for example, Taylor Branch: "The Case Against Foundations" in *The Washington Monthly* for July 1971 (vol. 3, no. 5).

Treasury may be poorer by $70,000, public causes are richer by $100,000.[6]

What are we to conclude from all this? Private foundation funds are not public funds or government money in the sense that the appropriations to HEW out of tax revenues are held and allocated by civil service staff employed by the government. They are as private as the endowment of Stanford University, the Menninger Clinic and the Metropolitan Museum of Art. Just as the trustees of those institutions have the responsibility of managing the funds in conformity with their respective charters, so the trustees of charitable trusts, which include foundations, have the clear obligation of carrying out the terms set forth in the founding instrument.

On the other hand, foundation funds, because they have been committed to the service of the public good, belong in the public domain. Trustees are servants of the public because the public are the beneficiaries of the foundation. In short, foundations and other charitable trusts are by their nature and purpose "clothed with the public interest." Here again Professor Katz says it succinctly and says it well: "The foundation is public because it devotes all its resources exclusively to educational, scientific, religious, charitable and other purposes and applies none of its resources to the pecuniary advantage of any person (other than regular compensation for service rendered). It is private in the sense that it is nongovernmental and derives its resources from gifts by private donors (or income from the investment of such gifts). *It is a privately organized public institution.*"[7]

Strict adherence to the terms of the charter so far as changing circumstances permit—that is clearly a trustee's duty. In that respect he is accountable to the donor. Equally clearly his duty is that of public servant, for he is accountable not only to the society he serves but to the legal and moral principles of trusteeship, which over recent centuries have set the standard by which his performance will be judged. The full implications of the private-public aspects of foundations are, as Alan Pifer said in the quotation which heads this chapter, far reaching. There is no need to emphasize the nongovernmental aspect, but unless the public aspect is fully recognized and accepted, foundations will be in danger. "What is at stake here," writes David B. Truman, president of Mount Holyoke College, trustee of the Twentieth Century Fund, and member of the Filer Commission, "is not fiduciary obligation in the usual sense of respect for the testamentary wishes of a donor, but rather the very possibility of the disposition of resources through autonomous bodies such as foundation boards. Unless the latter fully accept, and are seen to accept, the 'public servant' concept, they will be destroyed or taken over by the government."[8]

6. Those who naively accept the tax dodge argument are also inclined to follow the tax inequity line. If a $200,000 donor (70% tax bracket) gives 10% of his income, or $20,000, for some charitable purpose, it "costs" him only $6,000. If a $12,000 donor (14% tax bracket) gives 10% of his income, or $1,200, he "saves" only $324. To some this seems manifestly unfair; to others the differential in costs or savings is simply the reflex of the differential in progressive tax rates. For a discussion of the issue see *Giving in America,* chapter V, and the Bittker article in the *Tax Law Review* already cited.

7. *Op. cit.,* p. 10. Italics added.

8. Private letter to the author.

11

3 Programs by Design or by Default — The Trustees' Role

"Most foundation trustees and executives clearly do not know what they are doing, in the sense that they do not know the consequences of the decisions they make for the society in which we live."

ORVILLE G. BRIM, JR.

"Foundations change, like it or not. The fundamental issue is whether they will change by chance or for significant reasons. The latter comes about only through conscious effort."

FREDERICK deW. BOLMAN

OF THE MANY advantages which foundations offer as a form of philanthropy by no means the least is the opportunity to develop carefully planned and coherent programs. "Wealth is nothing new in the history of the world. Nor is charity. But the idea of using private wealth imaginatively, constructively, and systematically to attack the fundamental problems of mankind *is* new."[1]

Some examples are instructive. The Rockefeller Foundation was created in 1913 to further "the well-being of mankind throughout the world." The senior Mr. Rockefeller, however, was convinced that health was the key to well-being, with the result that the foundation concentrated in its early years on programs of science and medicine. The improvement of medical education throughout the world and the demonstration of the value of public health programs are monuments to

---

1. John W. Gardner in his review of fifty years of the Carnegie Corporation in the Annual Report for 1961.

13

a brilliant program of organized philanthropy. In contrast the trustees of The Ford Foundation, when finally geared up for action in 1950, adopted the report of the Gaither Committee which based its recommendations on the premise: "In the Committee's opinion the evidence points to the fact that today's most critical problems are those which are social rather than physical in character—those which arise in man's relations to man rather than in his relation to nature. Here, it was concluded, is the realm where the greatest problems exist, where the least progress is being made, and where the gravest threat to democracy and human welfare lies."[2] As a result the trustees focused on five areas of foundation concern: the problem of world peace, problems of democracy, problems of the economy, problems of education and the scientific study of man.

These are two examples of large general purpose foundations. It should be obvious that the larger the foundation, the more important it becomes to plan the program of philanthropy. A $5 million program of grants should have a far more significant impact than one of $5,000. And the more general the mandate of the foundation, the more imperative it is for trustees to select those areas of activity in which foundation support will concentrate. Not even the largest foundation can respond to all requests, however worthy and legitimate, without committing the mistake of "scatteration," that ever threatening blight to sensible philanthropy.[3] Broad general purposes are by no means the monopoly of the larger foundations, and it would be a serious mistake for the trustees of smaller foundations to ignore the need for clearly formulated goals on grounds that available funds are modest.

The trustees of special purpose foundations face the problem in somewhat different terms. In many cases the area of primary, if not sole, concern has been laid down by the donor. Thus the Longwood Foundation, founded by Pierre S. du Pont in 1937, with assets currently around $200 million, has as its primary obligation the support, operation and development of Longwood Gardens, a former du Pont estate near Kennett Square, Pennsylvania, and the largest horticultural gardens in the United States. The trust instrument (1924) of The Duke Endowment gives as its purpose: "To make provision in some measure for the needs of mankind along physical, mental, and spiritual lines"; but in fact Mr. Duke restricted the program to North and South Carolina and specified the exact percentage of income to be given to Duke University, to three other educational institutions, to private hospitals, to orphanages, to rural Methodist churches and to ministerial pensions.

In other cases, however, it has been the trustees who have designated the special objectives. Neither John nor George Hartford, who left their large holdings in the Great Atlantic and Pacific Tea Company to the

---

2. *Report of the Study for The Ford Foundation on Policy and Program,* published by The Ford Foundation, November 1949, p. 14.

3. Note the comment made by Henry Ford II in his letter of December 11, 1976, resigning after 33 years as a trustee of The Ford Foundation: "Another consideration that I believe requires more attention is the need to scale down activities to a level that reflects diminished resources. It seems to me that with half of the income, we still are addressing as many different problem areas as we did 10 or 15 years ago. I suspect that we are tackling some of these rather thinly and not too effectively."

Hartford Foundation, laid down any requirements as to program. The trustees were responsible for directing the program to medical research. The Independence Foundation in Philadelphia, a split-off from the old Donner Foundation, concentrates on the support of private secondary education as the result of deliberate trustee decision. However the special purposes may have been arrived at, the trustees must decide on programs for carrying them out. The Pardee Foundation of Michigan, for example, has as its goal to promote the cure and control of cancer. But cancer research is now a major national enterprise and to be effective the trustees must decide, in the light of what others are doing, what lines of investigation to support, by what means and through which scientists and doctors.

Family foundations vary in size and mandate. The Rockefeller Brothers Fund, with assets around $200 million, is a family controlled general purpose foundation. So are the Mary Reynolds Babcock Foundation and the General Service Foundation, both middle-sized. The vast majority of what we think of as family foundations, however, are quite small. They are apt to be open-ended—i.e., for charitable, educational, scientific, religious, cultural purposes—in order to provide maximum latitude for the charitable preferences of the donor. In many cases, though by no means in all, decisions are somewhat haphazard and largely personal. But even if small family funds are viewed chiefly as the extension of an individual's giving, the foundation provides an opportunity for planned decisions. With all due allowance for the value of the unplanned, imaginative, heart warming response to an unusual appeal, it is an opportunity which even in the smallest of foundations should not be wasted. It is easy to give money away; to give it away intelligently takes careful thought.

American corporations gave $1.2 billion in 1975 to a variety of charitable causes, and somewhat less than half this sum was channeled through the 1,500 company-sponsored foundations. Since the 1969 Tax Reform Act with its 4% excise tax on the net investment income of foundations provides a disincentive to giving via foundations as against direct corporate contributions, why does so much corporate philanthropy continue to flow through company-sponsored foundations? For those with substantial endowments the answer is clear, but they constitute a small fraction of the total number.[4] The Conference Board suggests a number of reasons. Foundations stabilize company giving by evening out the fluctuations in annual earnings. They provide better management by putting responsibility for corporate giving on the shoulders of designated staff and directors. They permit better program development by providing scope for long-range plans.

The best of the company-sponsored foundations are managed in a thoughtful, sensitive and responsible manner, with much care given to a

---

4. According to *The Foundation Directory*, Edition 5, there are 273 company-sponsored foundations (out of 1,500) with assets of $1 million or more or grant programs of $500,000. The largest in asset value is the Alcoa Foundation with $108 million. Asset value bears little relation to the amount of grants, however, since most of these foundations are conduits for the companies' current philanthropic funds.

carefully thought out and articulated program. The hundred or so companies in The Cleveland Plan, pledged to donate 1% of pre-tax income to higher education, are operating within a concerted plan. For 30 years the Dayton Hudson Corporation has given directly and through the Dayton Hudson Foundation 5% of taxable income for community improvement, thereby setting a standard of leadership for other companies, both in Minnesota and across the nation. The social philosophy behind the program is clearly stated in their 1975 annual report: "The goal of our charitable program is to improve the quality of life of all the people in the areas where we do business through contributions to social action programs and arts organizations.... Because of the overriding importance of local social problems, Dayton Hudson has placed high priority on supporting the search for their solution. Our emphasis continues to be on the critical needs of youth, the disadvantaged, and the residents of central cities.... Dayton Hudson supports the arts because we view them as a basic ingredient in our quality of life—an influence on virtually everything that gives flavor to our American experience. The creative people supported or inspired by arts institutions design our homes and cities, define and test our social values, and help to perpetuate the heritage of our citizens. The humanizing influence of the arts is keenly needed in all of our urban environments."[5]

Yet studies conducted by The Conference Board and others indicate that corporations have managed their programs of philanthropy less well than other aspects of their corporate affairs. Philanthropy tends to be viewed as a form of public relations. In most cases staffing is inadequate and planning limited. It will be a happy day when more corporations take their charitable obligations seriously and begin realizing the potential in their resources and planning capacity.[6]

The problem of program is both simpler and more acute for the board of directors or the distribution committee of community foundations. Many of the special funds and trusts which constitute the capital assets of the foundation will have designated purposes and beneficiaries, and all the resources are intended to serve the needs of a given community or region. How much simpler than the well-being of mankind throughout the world. But needs always exceed resources, especially in a period of major urban crisis. *Omnis determinatio est negatio,* said Spinoza, which means in this context that for every grant made ten others must be denied. The older and larger community foundations are well managed, and some of the newer ones exhibit considerable imagination and vitality. But others are struggling to achieve a program, badgered on the one side by a constant stream of heart-rending requests for help and handicapped on the other by a board not able or not willing to make the kind of decisions

5. *Contributions for Community Improvement for 1975,* p. 3.

6. See James F. Harris and Anne Klepper, *Corporate Philanthropic Public Service Activities,* November 1975, a study prepared for the Filer Commission; James F. Harris, *Corporate Philanthropy in the United States,* April 1975, a study prepared for a group of visiting Japanese businessmen; Elliott G. Carr, James F. Morgan and Associates, *Better Management of Business Giving,* Hobbs, Dorman & Company, 1966.

out of which a program is created.

The fundamental problems of mankind—to hark back to John Gardner's statement quoted at the beginning of this chapter—may not change, but the social, economic and political contexts in which they manifest themselves certainly do. Modern governments assume responsibility for health and welfare unimagined at the turn of the century. The rights of minorities are not yet fully realized, but at long last they have at least been recognized. Two World Wars, the creation of the United Nations, the mounting tensions generated by the cold war and the emergence of the Third World have produced an international pattern far different from that contemplated by Andrew Carnegie when he established in 1910 the Carnegie Endowment for International Peace. In its cumulative report covering the period 1954-70 the CBS Foundation commented:

> "Finally, the Foundation has recognized that public events and trends constantly develop new needs or suggest new priorities that can properly shift the emphases within corporate philanthropy from time to time. In the late 1950s, for example, following the evidence, presented by the first Sputnik, of the Soviet Union's advances in space exploration, there was new determination throughout the nation to strengthen our privately-supported educational institutions. In the 1960s, the widespread social unrest of the inner cities revealed a newly-felt need to support efforts directed at so solving or alleviating problems involving minority groups and urban life. Similarly, during the 1960s, the economic plight of institutions and programs in the arts demonstrated both the need and the appropriateness of increased corporate support in that field. The CBS Foundation, rather than adhering rigidly to a fixed and narrow definition of its purposes, has sought whenever possible to respond to such changing needs."

Thomas Parrish gives an amusing illustration in his essay, "The Foundations: 'A Special American Institution'." "According to some authorities, the first United States foundation was the Magdalen Society of Philadelphia, a perpetual trust which exists today as the White-Williams Foundation. Its aims have been somewhat modified from those it was given in 1800, which were 'to ameliorate the distressed condition of those unhappy females who have been seduced from the paths of virtue and are desirous of returning to a life of rectitude.' After more than a century of patient attempts to keep going in the face of the chronic insufficiency of unhappy females desirous of rectitude and of the frequent intractability of those who did present themselves, the trustees voted in 1918 to broaden the work of the foundation."[7]

Just as foundation trustees have the responsibility for setting the initial program directions of their foundations, so they have the further and continuing responsibility for keeping them up-to-date. A few examples of the way this can be done may prove helpful. The election of a

7. *The Future of Foundations*, p. 13.

arguing either that there is no need for a review since all is going well or that every meeting and every new grant are by their very nature reviews of program. "We review our program every time we make a grant," is the frequent response to the question, how often do you make a careful review of overall program. It is, of course, true that there are other ways of reviewing program besides a formal (and publicized) study, but it is well to heed Bolman's admonition: "Public and private distrust of foundations may arise in part because these tax-favored institutions neither police themselves *nor visibly exert themselves for renewal of purpose and performance.*"[12]

Good foundation practice requires in its own self-interest something more in the way of review than mere lip service. Effective management requires more. The shifting forces affecting public welfare require more. How often? Once every five years or at least once every ten would seem reasonable intervals for the kind of review here proposed. The world changes too fast for foundation trustees to live in the past.

12. Frederick deW. Bolman, "The Need to Evaluate a Foundation," *Foundation News,* January/February 1970, p. 20. Italics added.

4 The Hard Choice Among Public Needs

"Any individual can waste his substance in riotous living if he so chooses. . . . But if a foundation is to be true to the only proposition that can serve as a sound rationale for its existence, it simply does not have the liberty to waste its resources. No matter that foundations do not always live up to what they should stand for, the philosophy that undergirds them must maintain that they exist, along with government, to tackle and try to solve the major problems of the society."

MERRIMON CUNINGGIM

ALL FOUNDATION TRUSTEES face the problem of choice among competing requests for funds. Since there is never enough money to satisfy all public needs, trustees must decide which areas of human welfare are the proper concern of their foundations. Except for foundations with narrowly restricted purposes and for "supporting" foundations, the choice is legion and never easy.

To take a random example characteristic of a host of others, consider the problems faced by the trustees of the Eugene and Agnes E. Meyer Foundation (with assets of about $23 million and annual income of slightly over $1 million), which "is engaged in making grants for charitable, scientific and educational purposes in response to the changing needs of the Greater Washington metropolitan community." How does one best serve the needs of such a community with its explosive mixture of blacks and whites, rich and poor, cultured and impoverished, transients and indigenous? By supporting the Kennedy Center and the National Gallery which enrich the cultural life of the community and of the nation, or by funding health services for the poor, housing programs for the powerless, public interest organizations, and the like? There is no easy or simple answer.

One of the great virtues of foundations is their perpetuation of multiple choice in giving. A democratic society depends on pluralism. The free competition of the marketplace has its value for philanthropy as

21

well as for the exchange of goods. "There really is no other society in the world," commented Robert F. Goheen at a regional foundation conference in Los Angeles in November 1976, "where the university president with an important set of concerns or the social welfare agency with a critical set of needs can go and market those concerns and those needs to a variety of funding sources. And if they strike out with the first or second or third or fourth, they still may make it with the fifth. Then down the span of time the fifth may have been proved right to back them and all the others wrong." Any constraint, whether by law, threat of legislation or executive interpretation, on the freedom of trustees weakens the capacity of foundations to make their proper contribution to our society. Subject only to such restrictions and directions as are embodied in the instrument establishing the foundation or charitable trust, trustees must be free to decide as they think best and to select such public needs—educational, medical, scientific, cultural, religious, social—as they believe appropriate for their foundations and best for society.

The choices of foundation trustees are reflected in the distribution of foundation grants, and it is instructive to compare these with the pattern of total private philanthropy in the U.S. The following table shows this comparison in percentage figures:

	Total Private Giving in U.S. 1975	Foundation Grants 1975	1961-73
Religion	43.5%	2%	4%
Health	14.9	24	15
Education	13.3	26	32
Welfare	9.2	12	13
Arts & Humanities	7.2	9	9
Civic & Public	3.0		
International		11	14
Science & Technology		16	13
Other	8.9		
	100.0%	100%	100%

Differences in classification make strict comparisons difficult, but it is clear that education is the major recipient of foundation money and religion, which is the primary concern of individual giving, is least favored. Percentages vary from year to year, so that the figures for 1961-73 are probably most indicative of foundation interests. There has been no significant trend over these years, save for some decline in support for international activities.

From time to time critics of foundations have alleged that foundation money was being used to support subversive agencies or programs, partisan political activities or other improper objectives. Neither the Cox nor Reece Committees of the 1950s, however, uncovered anything of significance, and the Patman investigations in the 1960s found remarkably few examples. Indeed, the Peterson Commission, operating at the height of the controversy, in a stratified sample of 200 foundations found "first that only 1 percent of all foundations viewed any of their grants as controversial; second, that the grants involved amounted to only 0.1 percent of the total grants made between 1966 and 1968 and, as such, were almost totally centered in the large foundations."[1] Nevertheless, Patman and other members of Congress made the most out of the few instances they could find, characterizing all foundations with the faults of a few and creating the impression, temporarily and in some limited circles, that foundation trustees were engaged in various forms of political skulduggery. This accounts for various restrictive provisions respecting program in the Tax Reform Act of 1969—restrictions on grants to individuals, the requirement of "expenditure responsibility" for grants to organizations not listed by IRS as public charities, and special limitations on lobbying and partisan political activity.

Many, probably the majority of, trustees have not found these restrictions oppressive or inconvenient. According to a survey conducted by the Council on Foundations in 1974, 68% of the foundations sampled had never made grants to individuals and 61% had never given to non-501(c)(3) agencies or organizations which would have required under the provisions of the 1969 Tax Reform Act expenditure responsibility on the part of the foundation. And very few trustees have raised their voices in protest over the inroads on the right of free speech made by the special restrictions on lobbying and on political activity.[2] "A majority of foundations spend most of their funds on conventional projects and in conventional ways that are similar to the traditional patterns of individual giving," is the conclusion of the Peterson Commission.[3]

It is precisely this conclusion which gives rise to much current dissatisfaction with foundation performance. The litany of criticisms here ranges from those who speak for the underprivileged, the minorities, the "powerless," to the most reputable members of the philanthropic Establishment. Thus, the members of the Donee Group in their 1975 critique of the Filer Commission's Report indict foundations

1. Peterson Commission Report, p. 84.

2. Two trustees who have publicly and vigorously protested are John G. Simon in "Foundations and Public Controversy: An Affirmative View" in Heimann (ed.): *The Future of Foundations,* and Paul N. Ylvisaker in a study which he and Jane Mavity prepared for the Filer Commission, "Private Philanthropy and Public Affairs," and in an address to the Annual Conference of the Council on Foundations in May 1976 entitled "The Filer Commission in Perspective." It is worth noting that, while 32% of the foundations in the CF survey made grants to individuals before 1969, only 19% made such grants after the Tax Reform Act; and while 39% made grants prior to 1969 that would have involved expenditure responsibility, only 16% made such grants in 1970 and 20% in their most recent tax year. In some quarters at least the Act had a decidedly dampening effect.

3. *Op. cit.,* p. 86. In spite of that conclusion and the inhibitions of the 1969 Tax Reform Act, there continue to be those who view foundation performance with alarm. As recently as June 1976 Representative Larry McDonald of Georgia made a speech in the House of Representatives with the title "Beware the New Mandarin Class" in which he repeated the old canard: "By a policy of tax-exemption, private foundations are subsidized by the tax payers to engage in social experimentation with which the majority of tax payers clearly disagree." *Congressional Record* for June 29, 1976, p. E3669.

along with American philanthropy in general. "We believe that instead of being the venture capital for social change, philanthropy has, for the most part, patterned itself after its corporate and governmental counterparts. Most of it has become bureaucratic, safe and more conservative and less willing to take risks than the government."[4] At the other end of the spectrum John D. Rockefeller 3rd, reflecting on "the basic assumptions and directions of foundations in general" as he ended forty years of service as a trustee of The Rockefeller Foundation, commented:

> "The uncertainties and urgencies of our time make it essential for every institution concerned with public service to re-examine its approach. Foundations particularly must constantly strive to attain their full potential in helping to deal with the critical problems and issues that confront us.... *I think that most foundations are too cautious in their approach—too prone to concentrate their efforts in areas of the tried and proven.* There has never been a time in our history when we were confronted with problems of the complexity and magnitude that we are today. If these problems are to be resolved, I believe that every element of our society must do its part. To measure up to this challenge we in the foundation field must be willing to innovate, to take risks, to make mistakes."[5]

These are serious charges made by serious and concerned individuals. Foundations, as we have seen, are free from many of the constraints under which other institutions operate. They do not have to maintain a market for their products or a public which will provide annual operating expenses or a constituency which will keep them in office. They are indeed *sui generis,* and it has been their proud boast that they are innovative, experimental, risk taking. That is the claim. "For an institution that presumes to be society's conscience, gadfly, critic, and innovator," says Paul Ylvisaker, "private philanthropy's performance (even friends and practitioners will admit) has generally been less than bold."[6]

The criticisms, though often lumped together, are of two kinds. One is that foundation grants are *conventional* because trustees are conven-

4. Donee Group Report: *Private Philanthropy: Vital & Innovative? or Passive & Irrelevant?* 1975, p. 8. See also *U.S. Foundations and Minority Group Interests,* a report prepared by the U.S. Human Resources Corporation in June 1975 (Herman E. Gallegos, president and principal author); Thomas R. Asher: "Public Needs; Public Policy; and Philanthropy," an analysis of their treatment by the Filer Commission; and Sarah C. Carey: "Philanthropy and the Powerless," a study prepared for the Filer Commission.

5. *Foundation News,* November/December 1971, p. 237. The members of the Filer Commission share this view. "The Commission is concerned that the philanthropic process may not be fluid enough to respond to new needs as they emerge and are perceived.... The Commission believes that private giving should be constantly aware of and sympathetic to emerging needs, particularly of groups and causes in society that are least able to meet their own needs." p. 169.

6. "Private Philanthropy and Public Affairs," pp. III 13-14. For a quite different assessment see Young and Moore, *Trusteeship and the Management of Foundations,* pp. 65-84.

tional in their thinking, reluctant to venture into novel or untried fields, skeptical of young and untested organizations. The failure is lack of imagination. The other is that foundation programs are *conservative* because trustees represent the Establishment and inevitably reflect its values. They shy away from becoming involved in social and political experiments which challenge existing relationships. The failure is lack of courage or of social conscience or both.

The failure of imagination, it is alleged, shows up in the nature of too many foundation grants. It takes less time and thought to make a grant to the Metropolitan Museum of Art than to search out and support young and relatively unknown artists; to underwrite operating costs of the Minnesota Symphony Orchestra than to choose among the ever new, ever optimistic, always precarious dance groups and experimental theaters; to endow a new professorship than to fund an unorthodox approach to the problem of academic tenure. Also there is less risk of making mistakes. And besides, all these worthy institutions are badly in need of support. Foundation trustees have been frequently criticized—in the academic world at least—for demanding innovative projects, novel educational experiments, marginal additions to the total enterprise, when what was desperately needed was basic support—the provision of meat and potatoes or a loaf of bread, as it were, rather than a new kind of salad dressing. There is more than a little truth to this criticism. Pilot projects are fine, but who pays the bill on the morning after? The policy trustees should follow will be some mixture of the "safe" and the "risky," the prudent and the creative, to borrow Robert Greenleaf's language,[7] of continued support for projects dependent on such support and short run pilot projects which demonstrate whether a new and untried idea is viable. It would be salutary for every board of trustees to review its grants program in these terms. The chances are that in most cases the amount of money allocated to innovative and risky ventures would be quite small. Foundations can afford to gamble, and a record with no mistakes indicates a failure of imagination.

Let us turn now to the second and more difficult criticism, namely that foundations are failing to deal with the urgent social and political problems of an imperfect society and particularly of a society consciously struggling to achieve a greater measure of social justice. This is not a valid charge against all foundations by any means. The record of The Ford Foundation is outstanding, as is that of several other foundations both large and small. Sarah Carey lists 41 foundations which have made grants to help the powerless groups she discusses in her study. This accusation is, however, the central theme of Nielsen's critique of "the big foundations." It is a cardinal point with the Donee Group and those who share the Group's perspective. It led to the adoption at the 27th Annual Conference of the Council on Foundations of a resolution on "Foundations and Social Justice" which after referring to the truths set forth in the Declaration of Independence and their continuing challenge to our society states: "That organized philanthropy should recognize the

7. "Prudence and Creativity: A Trustee Responsibility," *Foundation News,* May/June 1974.

urgent obligation to help bring about constructive social change, in accord with our declared American principles, through activities aimed at increasing the options freely and fairly open to every individual and at improving the responsiveness of public and private institutions in working for the more complete realization of human rights for all our people."[8]

Social change as an abstract concept, however, is ambiguous, and in concrete terms it becomes highly debatable. The distinction is sometimes made between changing the system and change within the system. Insofar as the distinction can be maintained, it is hard to fault trustees for not waxing enthusiastic over proposals which threaten radical changes in the system. Why should they fund projects the purpose of which is to undermine the conditions which produced the foundation's assets? But where does one draw the line? Is it possible to do so in a universally satisfactory fashion? When Ralph Nader seeks to protect consumers against faulty merchandise, manufacturers view it as a threat to the system. Do environmentalists and conservationists protect the world we live in or do they ignore principles basic to American life? By no means do all politicians believe that Common Cause is improving rather than undermining our political system.[9]

We can all agree that our social, economic and political system is not perfect. There are unjustifiable inequalities of wealth. Justice is not the same for everyone. Equality of opportunity is an ideal rather than a fact. The powerless lack the ability and means to correct their situation. What can and what should foundations do about these inequities? Vernon Jordan, executive director of the National Urban League, reported to the Foundation Luncheon Group in New York City in June 1972 that, according to the *Foundation Grants Index,* in 1970 and 1971 less than 5% of dollars allocated to child welfare went to the black communities and of that only 0.5% went to black agencies; that less than 10% of grants for youth programs went to the black community and only 1% of that to black agencies; that only 3% of money given for assisting the aged went into the black community. *U.S. Foundations and Minority Group Interests,* already cited above, reports that in 1972-73 Spanish heritage groups, representing 5% of the total population, received 0.8% of foundation dollars; of 217 such grants only 39% went to agencies controlled by people of Spanish heritage. Americans of Asian descent, representing 0.6% of the population, received in 1972-74 0.1% of foundation money, with no more than 22% of that small sum channeled to agencies

8. See Waldemar A. Nielsen: *The Big Foundations,* chapter 21, and the Donee Group Report: *Private Philanthropy: Vital & Innovative? or Passive & Irrelevant?*

9. In an address to the Foundation Luncheon Group of New York Daniel P. Moynihan, now Senator Moynihan, cautioned foundation officers and trustees about becoming too political. "I believe there is a powerful set of motivations," he said, "some attractive, some less so, which more and more seek to politicize the activities of charitable foundations under the pretense of disinterested neutrality.... The activities of foundations are inescapably political, regardless of what Congress might desire or statutes might demand. The concern of foundations should be to be even-handed in the political consequences of those activities, seeking neither to advance nor impede any cause save that of understanding and competence." *Foundation News,* March/April, 1972.

managed by the minority groups represented.[10]

The July/August 1973 issue of *The Chicago Reporter,* published by the Community Renewal Society, carried an article on the pattern of giving by Chicago foundations to minority controlled agencies. Citing a survey by the Urban Dynamics/Inner City Fund of Chicago's 1,600 foundations, of which only 200 "exhibited some interest in minority civil rights and inner-city social problems," the article analyzes the 1972 grants of the city's five largest foundations. Out of a total of just over $15 million in grants $634,000, or 4.13%, went to minority controlled institutions. "By and large," writes the author, "foundation money goes to the tried and true. Chicago's wealthiest foundations—as is true of the nation's—usually support programs of established institutions. Innovative ideas or organizations lacking technical expertise in budgeting or proposal writing rarely get foundation support." The preference for white agencies in coping with minority and inner-city problems is clearly a sensitive point, which trustees would do well to consider.

In the light of these and other dismal data the charge of timidity against foundation trustees seems unavoidable. Sarah Carey in the study already referred to summarizes the situation. "Regardless of how the pie is sliced, there is no question that grants made directly for social change or to assist the powerless are dwarfed by the massive philanthropic contributions made annually in support of education, the arts, health services and the like.... The basic fact then is that philanthropy generally is not interested in supporting social activism or the interests of the powerless except, to a limited extent, through established institutions."[11] Carey, however, goes on to suggest that the situation is slowly, but perceptibly, improving. She points out that a few foundations like the DJB Foundation have committed capital as well as income to helping the underprivileged; that at least 41 foundations have shown an interest in social justice; that more foundations, especially the community foundations, are staying by their weaker recipients in order to keep them going; that more foundations are providing technical assistance as well as money; that more foundations are accepting expenditure responsibility for their recipients; and that a few new foundations have been recently created for the express purpose of supporting "groups which are too controversial or too risky to find funds at larger, more established funding sources."[12]

10. See footnote 4 for reference to *U.S. Foundations* etc. Jordan's data are in his address, "The Foundation and Society," given to the Foundation Luncheon Group on June 13, 1972.

11. "Philanthropy and the Powerless," pp. 5-7.

12. Vanguard Foundation Annual Report 1975, p. 3. The Vanguard Foundation was formed early in the 1970s by a group of young men and women, each of whom had substantial private means and was concerned over the distribution of wealth in our society. The Haymarket Peoples Fund was established in Boston two or three years later on similar principles. Their grants go to "groups and projects working to change the relations and distribution of power, as opposed to those treating only the surface manifestations of this unequal distribution." Annual Report 1975, p. 20. A third such foundation, Liberty Hill Foundation, has recently been set up in Los Angeles. Is the proposition that "wealth and power should be much more equitably distributed throughout the population," as the 1975 Annual Report of the Vanguard Foundation

In the light of these considerations, what can and what should foundation trustees be doing? A few generalizations may provide some guidance.

First, it is a central principle of our pluralistic society and our democratic system of government that men—including foundation trustees—should be free to make their own decisions within the context of what is good for society as a whole. Subject to such mandates as the donor or donors wrote into the governing charter, the trustees have not only the option of making, but the moral responsibility to make their own choices regarding the allocation of funds.

Second, the decision will depend in part on size. Experimental or innovative programs are likely to require more time and money than the majority of small family foundations have available—though here and there some creative individual will work wonders with slender resources. For the middle-sized and large foundations, programs of grants are likely to be a mixture of what Young calls supportive, developmental and innovative. Vanguard and Haymarket may go "all out," but most foundations will settle for a mixture.

Third, boards of trustees have been largely composed to date of people of wealth and their close associates. Their framework of values is largely set by their position in society. The ultimate question is whether enough of them can rise enough of the time above that framework and their own vested interest in maintaining the status quo to recognize the forces changing our social institutions and structure. Will enough of them recognize the claims of a changing set of public needs and be prepared to use some of the resources at their disposal to help a different world take shape? In highest terms this is the challenge of statesmanship—of the capacity to see beyond self to the good of all society.

It will also be a matter of prudence, for if too many people feel left out of the system, sooner or later they will seek to change the system. This is the stuff that revolutions are made of.[13]

---

affirms, intended to be a challenge to the system itself or a statement of the need for improving the way the system works?

13. See Thomas R. Asher, *op. cit.*, pp. 49-50, for a powerful statement of this position. Or listen to the rhetoric of Vernon Jordan in the address mentioned above: "It is obvious that the searing, urgent issues currently tearing at the fabric of our society, require for their resolution institutional changes that will enlarge the opportunities and the role of the neglected minority segments of our nation. These questions constitute a challenge of the first magnitude to the foundation community, a challenge that calls its very being into question. For if foundations refuse, either through fear or through misunderstanding, to try to resolve these burning issues, then they are truly a redundant and expensive luxury in our society."

5 How Far Should the Dead Hand Reach?

> "Conditions upon the earth inevitably change; hence, no wise man will bind trustees forever to certain paths, causes or institutions. I disclaim any intention of doing so. On the contrary, I give my trustees full authority to change policy or causes hitherto aided, from time to time, when this, in their opinion, has become necessary or desirable. They shall best conform to my wishes by using their own judgment."
>
> ANDREW CARNEGIE

A PERIODICALLY RECURRING controversy over foundation management is reflected in the question, to what extent should the donor and the donor's family exercise control over the investment of funds and the character of the program?

Trustee management of foundation assets has less than an unblemished record. In ten years of investigations Representative Patman uncovered a limited number of financial abuses, such as imprudent investments, inadequate payouts and improper self-dealing practices. Very few trustees and a very small percentage of foundations were involved, but their mistakes were blown out of all proportion and unfortunately tarnished the foundation image. The financial restrictions embodied in the Tax Reform Act of 1969 were designed to eliminate these abuses. While foundation involvement in family dominated companies has not been completely ended, it is on its way out, as foundations complete their divestiture of excess stock holdings. The old charges that foundations could be "manipulated" for the financial benefit of the donor and that they enabled the donor and his family to maintain control over the family business are no longer valid. There is no ground on this score for challenging control of foundations by the donor or his family. Current arguments, therefore, center on the extent to which it is either desirable or appropriate for the family to exercise control over the expenditure of funds.

For community foundations the issue is minimal. Members of the distribution committee (who in most cases constitute the governing board) are required to be broadly representative of the community, and they are normally appointed by outside public officials, institutional or organizational representatives and the trustee banks. It is not uncommon to consult the donor's wishes in trusts set up by a living donor and in "in-and-out" or "pass through" gifts where principal as well as income is distributed. Donors may designate fields, such as education or care for the aged, for support from their funds; or they may specify that the income go to the support of named institutions, such as a given church or hospital. But in all cases the distribution committee has the final decision and can deviate from the donor's instructions if the original purpose is no longer appropriate or viable.

Company-sponsored foundations are in an ambivalent situation. While they provide a number of advantages to the corporation, their greatest value is to the beneficiaries. By evening out good profit years and bad, corporations can maintain a steady level of grants—to the great advantage of agencies depending upon corporate support. Since most companies give directly out of their corporate resources as well as through their foundations, they could, without too much inconvenience to themselves, manage all their charitable giving as a direct expense item. So long as corporate philanthropy is viewed as a high level form of public relations, it is unlikely that the parent company, i.e., the donor, will give up control of distribution. A few corporations, however, are beginning to understand their social responsibility for the public good and the consequent desirability of more independent boards or committees of distribution.

The small family foundations—which dominate in numbers but not in assets—face special problems. Of the 24,925 foundations on which data are available, 18,349 foundations, or 73.2%, have assets of $200,000 or less and that 15,580, or 62.4%, have no more than $100,000 in capital assets. With a few exceptions these are in a quite literal sense the extension of individual giving. Most of them are relatively recent. There is as yet limited evidence as to what happens after the donor's death, though we do know that since 1969 there has been significant mortality among this group.[1]

The future of the small family foundation is uncertain. The requirements of the Tax Reform Act of 1969, particularly onerous in the

---

1. Precise data regarding the birth and death rates of foundations are hard to come by. Summaries of available information are to be found in John G. Simon's "Are Private Foundations an Endangered Species?" in *Foundation News*, January/February 1974 and in the *Revised Report and Recommendations to the Commission on Private Philanthropy and Public Needs* prepared by the Council on Foundations, August 1975, pp. III 25-34. In "An Analysis of Foundation Center Data on Creation, Dissolution and Reclassification of Private Foundations" prepared by Caplin & Drysdale and The Foundation Center office in Washington, the authors compare a Treasury list of 1,300 foundations in existence in 1962 with Foundation Center data for 1972. Using capital assets in 1962 of $100,000 or less as the criterion of smallness, they found that the small foundations constituted 34% of the sample. "Of the 'small' foundations 23 percent ceased to exist by 1972. Two-thirds of these terminations among 'small' foundations occurred in the three years surveyed during which the 1969 Act was effective. Clearly, many small foundations chose not to attempt to continue to operate under the new law."

case of small unstaffed foundations, may encourage the dissolution of these small entities through spending out of existence or merging with community foundations or in some other way. The 1969 Act, for example, carries a special provision by which a donor may create a fund, which then functions like a private foundation, but which has all the tax advantages of a public charity, on condition that all remaining assets will be turned over to public charities within one year of the deaths of donor and spouse.[2] Alan Pifer, president of the Carnegie Corporation of New York, suggested some years ago a division between private family charities and independent foundations. The former would enjoy relatively few restrictions respecting investments, family control, confidentiality, but their assets would be disposed of and the "charity" dissolved within ten years of the donor's death. Independent foundations would be subject to various restrictions regarding investments, full accountability and a majority of trustees not related to the family. Pifer does not propose a specific dividing line between the two classes in terms of asset size, but it is clear that he has the small family foundations in mind when he describes "private family charities."[3] Family foundations may die a natural death; they may at some future date receive a life sentence; or, like so many organizations in which people's emotions are centered, they may exhibit a remarkable capacity for survival. In any event, they represent too small a segment of the foundation world to justify concern over their natural tie to donors and to donors' families.

The issue of donor and continued family control over the charitable use of foundation money, therefore, focuses on the middle-sized and larger foundations, those with assets of $1 million or more. The current edition of *The Foundation Directory* lists 2,533 such foundations. These foundations hold 90% of all foundation assets and are responsible for 80% of foundation giving. In the light of the source of the money and the natural feeling that members of the family and trusted friends will be more sensitive than strangers to the donor's philanthropic interests, what are the arguments against the perpetuation of family control?

The first is a psychological argument directed primarily at the donor who, it is alleged, tends much too often to be arbitrary and high-handed in his philanthropic decisions. People with wealth sufficient to create foundations are usually strong-minded and successful individuals who are apt to be as decisive and independent in their giving as in their getting. In spite of his eloquent mandate conferring complete responsibility on the trustees, Andrew Carnegie ran the Carnegie Corporation from its inception in 1911 until he died eight years later. During the first three years of The Rockefeller Foundation John D. Rockefeller, Sr., reserved the right to allocate $2 million per year of income in accordance with his own wishes. More recently the decision of the trustees of The Danforth Foundation, announced in 1973, to make matching grants of $60 million to Washington University and $20 million to St. Louis

---

2. Section 170 (b)(1)(e)(3).

3. "The Foundation in the Year 2000," published by the Foundation Library Center, 1968, as Occasional Papers: Number One, pp. 9-10.

University was widely interpreted as an arbitrary exercise of family interests.[4]

The second argument is political and stems from the quasi-public character of foundations. Since they exist to serve the public good, it is important that they serve it well. Independent trustees drawn from a wider spectrum than the donor's immediate circle are more likely, it is alleged, to be aware of the wide range of public needs and to be more responsive to a systematic approach. The performance of some foundations where family members haggle over support for their individual interests lends some support to this view, but against this must be set the imaginative and thoughtful programs of many family controlled foundations. The criticism is probably a reflection of a latent suspicion of great wealth and fear of the power which great wealth creates. The danger of dynastic control of society by the control through money of men and institutions has haunted the common man since the days of the Revolution. This was the great cry of the populists at the time The Rockefeller Foundation was established. It underlay some of the hostility to foundations in the Congressional hearings of the 1960s. "The emotional force of the argument," writes Yarmolinsky, "in the popular and legislative dialogue is considerable. The argument goes also to the role of personal wealth in the formation of public policy, and for that reason it resonates powerfully with deep-seated popular attitudes."[5]

The proponents of foundations have their counter-arguments, and they begin with the flat assertion that there is no empirical evidence proving that independently managed foundations are better run than donor controlled foundations. No study along these lines has as yet been undertaken. Indeed, the subjective character of the criteria for such a comparison would make it suspect. Any knowledgeable foundation observer can cite his shining examples and his horror stories on both sides of the issue, and conclusions will differ according to the weight one puts on various examples. Under these circumstances the burden of proof would seem to rest with the critics.

Second, it is maintained that the greater interest and involvement in the foundation by the donor and his family are assets which should not be discarded. The donor brings drive and energy, imagination and creativity, to the foundation he creates. His children have a sense of family responsibility. As different generations join the board, there is built-in diversity of outlook and attitude. There is, moreover, evidence to support the contention that family controlled foundations are more venturesome and risk-taking than independently managed foundations. Furthermore, there is always the hope, not infrequently realized, that the continued involvement of the donor and his family will lead to additional gifts to the foundation. And finally, as the responsibilities and

---

4. The chairman of The Danforth Foundation, William H. Danforth, is also chancellor of Washington University. The Danforth board is dominated by members of the family. The president of the foundation and four other staff members resigned because of the trustees' position.

5. Adam Yarmolinsky: "Donor Control of Foundations," a paper prepared for the Filer Commission, February 1975, pp. 4-5.

liabilities of trustees increase, it may become more and more difficult to find good people willing to serve who are not connected in some way with the donor and his family.

A minor argument, but one that should not be minimized, is the importance of educating younger generations as good philanthropists. The proper handling of wealth does not always come easily; it needs to be learned, and what better way than by serving as a trustee of a family foundation?

Perhaps the strongest argument in favor of continued family control is based on incentive. Take away donor and family control, and one takes away one of the most important incentives to the formation of foundations. This is simply the way human nature works. Arnold Zurcher favors the exclusion of the donor, his family and people directly dependent upon him from serving on the board or staff of any foundation with assets of $2 million or more or annual grants of $100,000 and up; but he goes on to say: "There are those who will consider this a draconian prescription and would resist its application. They would argue—and persuasively—that donor influence often produces philanthropy as creative as any produced by a foundation independent, or largely so, of family control.... It can also be argued that, as long as we continue a predominantly capitalist country, and look to private largess to sustain much of our education and culture, we must continue to encourage the creation of family foundations, and allow donor management, if that is necessary to encourage creation of private foundations. If, in the case of very wealthy families, this results in some sort of family foundation conglomerate, that—so runs the brief—must be regarded as a necessary, if undesirable, effect of the broader policy of encouraging the creation of foundations."[6] Zurcher confesses that "there is merit in these contentions," though he believes the merit is outweighed by the disadvantages. Most people close to foundations are likely to see it the other way.

There is finally the argument that time and nature will take care of the problem. As one generation succeeds another, the original influence of the donor and founder will lessen until for all practical purposes his descendants will function in exactly the same way as a completely independent board. In a different version of the argument it is suggested that, given sufficient time, descendants will lose interest in the foundation which will, perforce, have to turn to non-family sources for trustees. One or the other of these developments would probably occur, given the sufficient time referred to above. Will American society wait patiently while the slow process of evolution takes place?

That is the hope of those who are opposed to any limitations on donor and family influence. In their book the situation is not nearly so bad as the critics allege, and the remedies proposed are worse than the disease. Encouragement of diversity is, as we have seen, one of the strengths of the foundation world; and diversity must allow for the quixotic and capricious as well as for the sober and sensible. That is the price of a free society.

6. Arnold J. Zurcher: "Family Foundation 'Conglomerates'—What Should We Do About Them?" in *Non-Profit Report*, April 1974, p. 13.

A second approach is mandatory regulation by government. In its thoughtful and generally sympathetic report in 1965 "the Treasury Department recommends that provision be made to convert private foundations, after they have been in existence for 25 years, to management which is independent of their donors and parties related to donors." Ten years later in their critique of the Filer Commission's Report, "the Donee Group recommends a phase out of donor control over charitable organizations. Specifically, the governing boards of all foundations would be required by law to have no less than one third public members immediately and no less than two thirds public members after five years. Public members would be defined negatively to eliminate donors, their relatives and business associates."[7] The length of time necessary for effecting the desired changes and the degree of reduction of donor control will vary from one advocate to another, but the common theme of these and similar proposals is the conviction that only government regulation will bring about any significant reduction in donor and family control over foundations. It remains to be seen whether this conviction is correct or not, but whether right or wrong, strict governmental regulation of this kind would in the view of most knowledgeable foundation watchers greatly reduce, if not virtually eliminate, the creation of new foundations as well as decimating those now in existence.

Between a policy of letting nature take its course and one of immediate governmental regulation of all foundations lies a number of intermediate proposals. Zurcher would distinguish foundations by size, ignoring family control of the smaller ones and eliminating family members completely from the boards of the larger ones. Pifer, frankly concerned over the proliferation of small foundations, especially during the 1950s and 1960s, would, as we have seen, read them out of the foundation field but allow them considerable freedom of operation and control, while prescribing strict standards of operation, including less than 50% family membership, for foundations proper.

Another and milder form of this type of proposal was made by the members of the Filer Commission who, recognizing the validity of the criticisms based on social equity and possible limitation of access, nevertheless thought that there were counterbalancing arguments. Rather than proposing legislation to limit family control, the commission recommended the creation of a new legal category of independent foundations. "Governing boards of such foundations would be restricted to at most a minority representation by the donor, the donor's family and

---

7. *The Treasury Department Report on Private Foundations,* p. 56. The Report suggests that for foundations already in existence for 25 years an additional 5 to 10 years be allowed. It further proposes that "participation of the donor and related parties on the foundation's governing body should be fixed no higher than 25 percent." The Donee Group's arguments are to be found in *Private Philanthropy: Vital & Innovative? or Passive & Irrelevant?,* pp. 17-18. Some members at least of the Donee Group have recognized that their prescription of two-thirds nonfamily membership within five years is unrealistic. In the "Statement of Principles and Objectives of the National Committee for Responsive Philanthropy" (the successor group) the five year recommendation is changed to read "and no less than two-thirds public members within a reasonable time."

business associates." As incentive to the adoption of such status, independent foundations would be freed from the restrictive tax provisions on deductibility of gifts which under the Tax Reform Act of 1969 make private foundations second class citizens.[8] This formula has two great advantages: it avoids the arbitrary distinction between types of foundations based on size of assets, and it leaves the decision to limit donor and family control to the donor and his family. It is the principle of the carrot rather than the stick.

Except for doctrinaire populists the real issue is not who controls the foundations, but how good are their programs. Foundations should be judged, it is argued, on their performance. If trustees fail to maintain proper standards, they should be censured and their foundations subjected to appropriate penalties, the most drastic of which might be dissolution. This is good theory, but will it work in practice? Those who take this approach are advocating self-regulation. This can range from the establishment of standards of good practice, to which foundations will be encouraged to adhere, to the creation of a foundation accrediting agency which would police its members.

The notion of self-regulation through accreditation has intrigued a number of foundation commentators. The idea keeps popping up, only to be knocked down each time. Accrediting agencies with implicit policing powers function well in education, health, social work and other fields. Why not also for foundations? Mortimer Caplin, former Commissioner of Internal Revenue, urged a program of self-policing on foundations in an address to the Foundations Luncheon Group of New York in 1964. In 1969 the Council on Foundations, the Foundation Center and the National Council on Philanthropy jointly formed a special committee which drew up a list of nine criteria for a properly managed foundation and proposed a permanent oversight committee with responsibility for (1) the evaluation of foundations upon request, (2) periodic publication of a list of foundations having met the required standards, (3) the investigation of foundations which appear to be in violation of approved standards, (4) the establishment of appropriate procedures for conducting investigations, and (5) the refinement of standards as a result of experience and variations in standards appropriate to different types of foundations. In 1974 Lawrence M. Stone, Professor of Law at the University of California, Berkeley, proposed a Foundation Evaluation Board with supervisory powers in a study prepared for the Filer Commission.[9]

In spite of the storm signals raised by Patman's investigations of the

8. *Giving in America*, pp. 172-3. In a dissenting opinion two members of the commission say that the status of independent foundation should be granted only when the donor and his family are completely removed from the governing board, p. 220.

9. Caplin's recommendation is to be found in a reprint entitled "A Code of Practice Is Needed" from the *Proceedings of the Seventh Biennial Conference on Charitable Foundations,* New York University, 1965. The report of the Temporary Committee on Foundation Standards is in *Foundation News* for November/December 1969, pp. 213-5. Stone's proposal is in a paper entitled "The Charitable Foundation: Its Governance." See also for a review of these and related proposals Manning M. Pattillo: "Foundation Administration: Standards and Requirements" in the *Proceedings of the 10th Biennial Conference on Charitable Foundations,* 1971, pp. 77-87.

1960s, Caplin's warning and recommendation produced no concrete results. The report of the Temporary Committee on Foundation Standards, although approved by the boards of all three agencies, was stillborn. The Filer Commission did not endorse Stone's proposal. Recurring suggestions at foundation conferences or in publications along similar lines usually receive short shrift. Why? The advocates of some form of self-regulation with teeth are clearly in the minority. The rugged individualists among foundation trustees are the majority. But even those who would welcome the imposition of standards are stymied by the problem of sanctions. Colleges must be accredited to get their students into approved graduate schools. Hospitals need accreditation to qualify for Medicare and state aid. Public charities are greatly helped in their annual fund raising by the approval of the National Information Bureau. Foundations, however, have no need for any of these external symbols of approval. Their only threat is the danger of government regulation if they do not put their own houses in order.

Self-regulation through the development of desirable standards and constant encouragement to foundations to live up to such standards, however, is another matter. Andrews drew up in 1963 a code of practice containing eighteen criteria, only to have it vetoed by the board of the Foundation Center upon the insistence of one of the large foundations. In 1970 the Council, the Center and the National Council on Philanthropy again appointed a joint Committee on the Foundation Field headed by John W. Gardner, former president of the Carnegie Corporation. The committee made a number of excellent recommendations, including the development of voluntary standards of good practice. The committee expressed the view "that the policing function is not one which foundations are equipped to perform, or would find it in their interest to perform at this time.... We favor a broad membership organization which would work positively to develop professional standards appropriate to each type of foundation."[10]

The Foundation Center and the Council on Foundations have between them carried out many of the recommendations of the Gardner Report. In particular the Council has sought to define and promulgate criteria of good foundation practice. The Council's board has adopted various statements which have been made public in *Foundation News* respecting general principles, public information, the desirability of foundation concern for social justice and the like.[11] *Foundation News* continues to publish articles which both inform and encourage trustees with respect to their responsibilities. The programs of annual conferences invariably touch on these problems. The Council's membership, however, is far from universal. While its authority is growing, its clout is still mild. It is the major voice of the foundation world, however, and in time it may succeed

10. See F. Emerson Andrews: *Foundation Watcher*, Franklin and Marshall College 1973, pp. 263-6, for his account of the drafting of the code and its eighteen standards. The "Gardner Report," dated April 15, 1970, is available in mimeographed form from the Council on Foundations.

11. See *Foundation News* (or reprints) for January/February and March/April 1973 and the Council on Foundations' *Regional Reporter* for June 1976.

in raising and maintaining standards which all foundations will feel obligated to respect. Let us hope that this will be the case, for some form of self-regulation may be the price of survival.

These considerations lead to a series of uncomfortable conclusions with which trustees, and the foundation world in general, must make their peace. There are no compelling reasons for limiting immediate control by the donor over his foundation. It was his money. He did not have to channel his philanthropy through a foundation. To exclude him from a voice in the distribution of grants would seem to most people both inhuman and unfair, and in the nature of the case his voice is likely to be the dominant one.

There are, however, some reasons for limiting indefinite family control, but the social cost of such limitations may be greater than the benefits. The foundation assets never belonged to the descendants as they did to the donor, and family members of boards are not always picked for their competence, although there are outstanding examples to the contrary. The long tradition of popular opposition to anything which smacks of continued dynastic control of power—an attitude forged by the conditions under which our nation was formed and fed by the circumstances of its growth during the nineteenth century—makes the perpetuation of family control politically hazardous. This hazard might be met by some system of self-regulation by which foundations were held to approved standards, by some reclassification of foundations along lines suggested by Zurcher or Pifer, or by the Filer Commission's formula of providing tax and other incentives to become foundations independent of family control.[12]

Most people would agree that self-regulation is preferable to governmental regulation, both because the latter has a tendency to overkill and because it so often becomes an encroachment on the independence and diversity of foundations so essential to their contribution to society. Some sort of self-regulatory board or agency may ultimately be established, though knowledgeable observers such as Donald Young insist that foundations are too diverse to admit of a uniform code or single set of standards. It may be wise, however, to listen to the reflective judgment from Capitol Hill. "Responsible and respected citizens," says Senator Alan Cranston of California, "are genuinely concerned by the failure of foundations to regulate themselves adequately.... There have been a number of reasons advanced as to why foundations cannot regulate themselves—because of their diversity in size and function, because of the dichotomy between foundations which function in only one area and those which serve the

12. Carl Gerstacker in the article referred to in chapter 1, "Let 'Outsiders' Control Family Foundation Boards," argues from the "quasi-public" character of foundations against continued family control. "I have two reasons for urging this. In the first place, I think the best quality of trustees is usually found outside the family.... Another reason is even more compelling. In brief, I'm convinced that if we do not move to bring in a majority of outside trustees to our foundation boards, whatever their size, then the government will move to force us to do this. The trend is in this direction, and it is not time for us to stand by the seashore, like King Canute, and try to stop the tide." *Foundation News*, September/October 1975, p. 17.

general welfare in a variety of fields, and finally because it is not good manners for one foundation to criticize another. I must confess that these kinds of arguments are not helpful to the cause of foundations. They are not convincing to the American public, and they are not convincing on the Hill."[13]

Too many trustees unfortunately are not yet sensitive enough to political currents and social demands to recognize and accept what is in their best long term interests. Under the circumstances the most practical alternative is to make it so attractive to foundations to give up family control that the middle-sized and large foundations (at which the arguments of this chapter are primarily aimed) will voluntarily adopt the independent status recommended by the Filer Commission. This will involve some change in the law, but the change involves the removal of certain present restrictions, not the imposition of new ones.

Time will help, as noted earlier, though some family loyalties run long and deep. Mandatory retirement requirements based on age and mandatory limitations on the number of years of consecutive service would have a more immediate effect. There are strong arguments for such requirements, as we shall see in a later chapter. They would by no means eliminate family control, but they would reduce it, and they are probably the most palatable restrictions which foundation trustees might impose on themselves at the present time.

13. *Foundations on Trial*, published by the Council on Foundations, 1970, pp. 4-5. See also the trenchant observations of Harold M. Keele, former general counsel to the Cox Committee, in an article entitled "Unpublished Proceedings of New York University's Ninth Biennial Conference on Charitable Foundations," pp. 22-3. Young's position is set forth in *Trusteeship and the Management of Foundations*, p. 148.

6 The Virtues of Diversity

"The trustees...have the ultimate decision-making powers over what grants are to be made or withheld. Their general orientations are thus the major determinants of the foundation's policies and its impact on the cultural scene. That is, they are important gatekeepers of ideas."

LEWIS A. COSER

WHILE THERE ARE strong differences of opinion on the propriety of continued donor or family control of foundations, there is much less argument over the merits of greater diversity among foundation trustees. Whether based on a demand for broader representation of the diverse segments of American society or for greater sensitivity to the changing needs of that society, most commentators on the foundation field would agree with the Council's recommendation to the Filer Commission that "foundations should make a special effort to recruit board members and staff from groups not traditionally represented."[1]

We do not have anything like a complete social, economic and political census of the 100,000-130,000 trustees of the 26,000 foundations in the United States. Over the past 40 years a number of studies have been made, based on a sampling of trustees with some skewing toward the larger and better known foundations. These give us some data, which

---

1. *Op. cit.,* p. VI-2. See also the Peterson Report, pp. 89-90; the Filer Commission Report, pp. 170-1; the Donee Group Report, p. 19. For a dissenting view see the remarks of Professor Don K. Price, trustee of the Twentieth Century Fund and former vice president of The Ford Foundation, in the *Proceedings of the Second Biennial Conference on Charitable Foundations,* New York University 1955, pp. 207-8. Noting the charge that foundation boards are unrepresentative and too conservative and the argument that they should be composed of people representing various economic interests and minority groups, Professor Price says: "I do not think that these are the relevant criteria in establishing the role of the foundation trustee.... It seems to me ... that the absolutely essential function of a trustee is to bring to bear on policy problems the kind of judgment that a man can give only if he is not working for the foundation, only if he comes to it with status in other walks of life and, accordingly, with a quite general judgment about foundation business."

have changed remarkably little in four decades. The following table compares their findings.

	Lindeman (1930 data)	Coffman (1930 data)	Andrews (1952 data)
No. of foundations	70	55	20
No. of trustees	140	282	202
Average age	56.7	58.2	58
No. under 40	2	9	9
No. over 70	15	41	24
Percent over 70	10.7	14.5	12
No. over 80	3	6	9
No. of women		7	14
Percent of women		2.5	7

A high percentage in the three studies were Protestants—Episcopalians and Presbyterians accounting for 50%-57.5% depending on the study. Roughly one-third in each study were businessmen; 15%-20% were lawyers. Forty percent attended Harvard, Yale, Columbia or Princeton, and the great majority lived on the Eastern seaboard. The Peterson Commission survey in 1969 of 25 of the largest foundations found that 50% of the trustees had attended Ivy League colleges, and two-thirds had business, banking or legal connections. Lindeman's classic description of the 1930s remains all too true. The typical foundation trustee is:

> "... a man well past middle age; he is more often than not a man of considerable affluence, or one whose economic security ranks high; his social position in the community is that of a person who belongs to the highest income-receiving class of the population; he is, presumably, 'respectable' and 'conventional' and belongs to the 'best' clubs and churches, and he associates with men of prestige, power and affluence. His training has been largely in the arts and humanities and he possesses only a slight background in the sciences and technologies. He resides in the Northeastern section of the United States and has attended one of the private colleges in that region. His 'intelligence' is ranked high by various institutions of higher learning from whom he has received signal honors. He receives his income primarily from profits and fees. In short, he is a member of that successful and conservative class which came into prominence during the latter part of the nineteenth and early twentieth centuries, the class whose status is based primarily upon pecuniary success."[2]

Why so great a discrepancy between current thinking about the composition of foundation boards and the prevailing character of the majority of trustees? One reason is that the shift from passive

2. Eduard C. Lindeman: *Wealth and Culture,* Harcourt, Brace & Co. 1936, pp. 44-46. See also Harold C. Coffman: *American Foundations: A Study of Their Role in the Child Welfare Movement,* YMCA New York 1936; and F. Emerson Andrews: *Philanthropic Foundations,* Russell Sage Foundation 1956, chapter 3.

acceptance of control by those in authority to an active demand for broader participation in decision-making processes—a shift which is affecting all institutions and traditional patterns—is a fairly recent phenomenon. Change of this kind comes slowly, for it upsets long accepted relations. Resistance is strong, as the donor expects and intends through the selection of trustees to perpetuate control over "his" foundation. The self-perpetuating character of most boards makes it natural for trustees to select people of their own ilk, i.e., people of comparable standing in the community, people who will think alike rather than creating controversy by introducing different and possibly conflicting viewpoints. Where is one to find these representatives of different, even "alien," sectors of society? Those who seek to hold on to the conventional "collegial" pattern cite the lack of clear evidence that diversified or independent boards do in fact perform better than small closely-knit boards of bankers, lawyers, educators and people of wealth.

Lindeman's profile of the typical trustee is no longer accurate in all respects. Foundation trustees are no longer so highly concentrated along the East coast. The expansion of science and technology in the past half century has undoubtedly affected the educational background and intellectual orientation of the successful businessman trustee. Furthermore, a slowly increasing number of foundations, including some of the middle-sized family foundations and particularly some of the leaders like Ford, Rockefeller and Carnegie, have made conscious efforts to broaden and diversify their board membership by adding women, blacks and individuals chosen from non-power segments of society. A few, like Vanguard and Haymarket, have added members from the recipient groups. Coffman found less than 3% women in his sample of trustees in 1930; Andrews, only 7% women trustees in his 1952 study. A 1976 poll conducted by the recently formed Planning Committee for Women in Foundations increased that to 19%.[3]

Comparative data are not available to document a similar change in the membership of minority groups on boards of trustees. It is generally agreed that there has been some improvement in the number of black trustees in the last few years. In 1974 the Association of Black Foundation Executives undertook a survey of selected foundations revealing 4.5% of their trustees to be black.[4] *The Chicago Reporter* found only one black trustee among the 52 directors of Chicago's five largest foundations in a 1973 survey; in a 1976 repeat it found three black trustees out of a total of 45. Herman E. Gallegos, president of the U.S. Human Resources Corporation, believes himself to be the only Mexican-

3. Leeda Marting: *Women in Foundations,* mimeographed 1976. Out of 438 foundations replying to the questionnaire 4% had no male trustee and 34% no woman trustee; 10% had two or less male trustees, whereas 80% had two or less female trustees. See also Janet Oliver's article, "Women in Foundations Are Challenging the Status Quo," in *Foundation News* for July/August 1976.

4. Robert W. Hearn: "Foundation Trustees: The Need for Diversity" in *Foundation News* for November/December 1974. The smallness of the response—139 foundations or only 6% of those queried—throws some doubt over the results. On the assumption that foundations with black trustees would be more likely to respond the figure of 4.5% may be high.

American to be a trustee of any foundation and knows of only one Asian-American who is a trustee.[5] We have a long way to go.

A lot of nonsense has been written on the subject of participatory democracy, on the representation of all groups in the decision-making process, on giving beneficiaries, actual or potential, a voice in the allocation of grants. It is, therefore, important to understand why some diversification of foundation boards is desirable. The central and basic reason is that differences of viewpoint, properly presented, considered and synthesized, can lead to wider choices and better decisions. Whether it be a choice among public goods, a choice among methods for achieving some public good, or a choice among individuals and agencies to be supported, two heads are likely to be better than one, especially if each brings a different experience and perspective to bear on the decision. Industry is discovering that workers frequently have helpful ideas. Colleges and universities learned in the 1960s that students had something to contribute to shaping the educational program. Hospitals are improving their procedures as a result of listening to nurses and patients and staff as well as to doctors. Collective decisions can be wrong, but collective decisions representing the synthesis of diverse viewpoints are more likely to be right than decisions taken from a single perspective.

A second reason is accessibility. The most monolithically structured foundation can be readily accessible to all and sundry if it so decides. But the social and economic status of the majority of trustees together with their natural preoccupation with their own particular interests and concerns have in fact tended to make many foundations less accessible to the general public than should be the case with institutions presuming to serve the public welfare. This is the burden of the criticism of both the Filer Commission and the Donee Group leading to their recommendations, one voluntary and the other mandatory, that foundations seek more diversified boards. Different perspectives provide a wider range of sensitivity to human and societal needs.

And finally, there is the political or pragmatic argument. The modern temper is suspicious of elite organizations, of what appears to be irresponsible power. Foundations are suspect on both counts. The Peterson Commission concludes from its analysis of foundation trustees that "these boards clearly lack the kind of diversity that could further enlarge their perceptions about the raw surge of American life—a diversity, moreover, that could help establish a firmer public footing beneath the foundations at a time when they are involved in activities of great public sensitivity." And in their recommendations for the future the members of the commission suggest "that added diversity could have

5. Interview with author. See also *U.S. Foundations and Minority Group Interests*, prepared by the U.S. Human Resources Corporation and published in June 1975. Msgr. Geno Baroni, president of the National Center for Urban Ethnic Affairs and a member of the Donee Group, has been an eloquent spokesman on the under-representation of ethnic groups in the higher echelons of both profit and nonprofit institutions. See his testimony before the Subcommittee on Foundations of the Senate Committee on Finance for May 13, 1974, *Hearings etc.*, Government Printing Office, pp. 4-19; and also "The Power Structure Explored from an Ethnic Perspective" by Geno Baroni and Charles Conconi in *Foundation News* for January/February 1976.

two advantages. It might provide added perspective to the insights of the boards. This would be valuable in view of the enormous range of new problems our society faces. Also, it might allay some of the public suspicion of privatism and disdain. There is an obvious contradiction in claiming to represent the interests of pluralism in our society and yet practicing monism in the selection of trustees."[6]

The idea of greater diversity on boards does not entail, as it is sometimes thought to do, either the notion of "representation" or the concept of publicly elected members. Let us examine these in turn. Advocates of change in foundation structure sometimes talk as if foundation boards should be composed of representatives of women, minority groups, ethnic groups, the poor, the powerless, the beneficiaries, indeed, almost any distinguishable segment of society. Apart from the sheer impossibility of including representatives from all groups, the result would be boards of large size, of strongly conflicting interests, of political maneuvering, of confrontation, and finally of resolution by compromise. However appropriate or inevitable these characteristics may be to the political scene, their reverse is desirable for private boards. A trustee does not "represent" anyone. He has responsibilities, as we have seen, both to remain true to the terms of the trust, so far as circumstances will permit, and to safeguard the best interests of the beneficiaries of the trust. Integrity and impartiality, intelligence and commitment, are the hallmarks of the good trustee.

Is it not a contradiction in terms, it will be asked, to propose board members from diverse groups in society and to deny that they should represent the interests of those groups? The answer involves a subtle but important distinction. Experience, sensitivity, perspective are not the same as advocacy and special pleading. We know that to be true in our own lives; and since we cannot experience all things, we need to supplement our limitations with the experience of others. Eugene C. Struckhoff, vice president of the Council on Foundations, has stated the position in clear and simple language:

> "Every member of a board has a duty to speak to overall public interest and not for a single interest. In reality, however, each member brings to the board perceptions of priority and morality grounded in her or his life experience and condition. Boards composed only of white Anglo-Saxon Protestant males with backgrounds in business affairs and drawn from more affluent socio-economic groups do not mean to speak only or substantially for WASPS. They may intend the public welfare; but they are handicapped in achieving it in not being exposed to the aspirations and perceptions of the many constituencies they should serve. The member of a racial minority or other group will labor under a like disability in achieving the theoretical ideal of representing only the overall public interest. The rationale for a board drawn from diverse elements is grounded in the irrefutable fact that no one can get out of his skin. Theory and reality are not at war in this instance. It is,

6. *Op. cit.,* pp. 90, 138.

indeed, bad policy for a board member to regard himself as speaking *for* a constituency; but it is both inevitable and right for her or him to speak *as* a member of a group."[7]

The notion of "public members" on the boards of private or independent foundations is as recent and controversial as proposals for public members on corporate boards. Most private nonprofit organizations have self-perpetuating boards. A family foundation may co-opt an outside or "public member," but this is quite different from the election or appointment of one or more trustees by an outside agency. The case for greater diversity does not presuppose any such imposition. Nor does it require, as the Donee Group recommends, that diversification will be mandated by law. Indeed, the weakness of governmental intervention at this point is the difficulty of devising an adequate formula to cover all cases. Public members are clearly more important in large foundations than small ones. Where draw the line? Some foundations have large boards; some, small. How accommodate the number of outside members to variations in board size? What procedures would be effective in selecting and appointing public members? And why, if this is a proper policy for foundations, should it not also be applied to colleges and universities, hospitals and museums, the whole panoply of private nonprofit organizations? This would seem to be an area where private initiative based on good sense and what Aristotle called practical wisdom should bring about the desired changes.

Community foundations are in a class by themselves. They enjoy the advantages adhering to "public charities" partly because they have multiple sources of funds and partly because they are presumed to be responsive in special ways to the needs of their communities. Most community foundations do have public members since all or some of their governing boards (or distribution committees) are appointed by outside agencies or individuals; and in most cases these outside "electors" have been designated in such a way as to encourage the presence of individuals of diverse backgrounds and interests on the board. That, at least, is the theory. In practice members of the boards or distribution committees of community foundations have tended to reflect the same socio-economic characteristics to be found on the boards of many private foundations. This has been due in part to the need to give stature and status to the community foundation, in part to a certain casualness on the part of the appointing individuals and agencies, in part no doubt to the availability of people willing and able to donate the necessary amount of time, for community foundation trustees are among the hardest working members of the foundation world.[8] There are

7. *The Handbook for Community Foundations,* Council on Foundations 1977, chapter VII, section 1.11(3).

8. "In the understandable push to broaden boards it would be counter-productive to forget that an agency whose goal is accumulation of capital is benefited by the presence on the board of some members who have accumulated it," writes Struckhoff in the excellent *Handbook for Community Foundations,* chapter VII, section 1.11(1). He presents a thoughtful analysis and set of recommendations for the selection of community foundation trustees.

relatively simple ways in which community foundations can correct or improve the breadth of viewpoint to be found on their boards, and enough has been written on the subject to obviate the necessity of going into more detail here. The fallacy of thinking one must represent the interests of the appointing agency or office is a danger that must be more carefully guarded against. The success of the community foundation, or at least of the best of them, makes clear that neither self-perpetuation nor uniformity of interest and outlook is essential for effective board operations.

There are, of course, ways of introducing diversity of viewpoint without changing the composition of the board. Some foundations employ advisers on either a temporary or relatively permanent basis—a practice which is fairly common among special purpose foundations. Others will establish a program committee of nontrustees to make recommendations on grants. The use of ad hoc committees or outside experts to review overall program is yet another way of enriching trustee thinking with different viewpoints and ideas. Such methods are to be encouraged, for they reduce the danger of too limited a perspective on serving the public welfare.

Nevertheless, greater diversity on governing boards themselves is highly desirable. With their professed concern for the communities where their plants and employees are located company-sponsored foundations would do well to add one or more non-company and community-knowledgeable individuals. Every small family foundation could profit from the advice of at least one non-family member—an individual selected by the family to challenge their individual decisions, to suggest alternative outlets for their generosity, to "keep them honest" in their concern for society. Many of the large foundations have already diversified their boards. The others and the middle-sized foundations would do well to follow their example. Some mandatory limit on length of service, which will be discussed in more detail in the next chapter, would facilitate the process.

In terms of serving the public interest and in terms of safeguarding the future of private foundations greater diversity in board membership is required. This is one step which trustees could and should take on their own volition, and the time to take it is now.

7 The Responsibility of Trustees for Trustees

"A self-perpetuating board may well achieve a kind of self-satisfied insularity that almost defies attention to fundamental change in the conditions appropriate for sensible policy."

WILBERT E. MOORE

"Experience is the revelation in the light of which we substitute the errors of age for the errors of youth."

AMBROSE BIERCE

ALL FOUNDATION BOARDS face the problems of continuity and change in membership. Self-perpetuation is the most widely used procedure, although this is the exception rather than the rule among community and company-sponsored foundations. Some provision needs to be made and careful thought given to the selection of successor trustees—in short a plan of succession and a set of criteria for membership.

There are various ways in which individuals are appointed or elected trustees. The initial board is usually selected by the donor and, while he or she is alive and active, his or her voice is likely to be decisive in the selection of successor trustees regardless of what formal device has been adopted. Indeed, the donor can direct or control the future selection of trustees after his death by restrictions in the charter. The Duke Endowment provides an example. Through the trust indenture establishing his foundation James Duke specified that the self-perpetuating board of fifteen should always contain a majority of natives or residents of North and South Carolina and that his daughter, Doris Duke, should be made a member upon reaching the age of twenty-one. By selecting as the first board a group of individuals chiefly associated with the Duke power interests and by requiring that the assets of the foundation be invested in the Southern Power System securities, he made practically certain that the board would continue to be dominated by individuals representing his business interests.[1]

In some foundations, particularly of the charitable trust variety, trustees are officers of the bank or trust company managing the corpus, or individuals appointed by the institutional trustee. In other cases where a highly trusted lawyer has been named by the donor to the original board, practice if not prescription has led to the selection of younger partners of the law firm to succeed their seniors. A variation of this "hereditary" practice occurs when, by specific provision or by preference, a son or daughter of a trustee is nominated to succeed the father.[2] Appointment may, of course, be made by some outside agency or institution, as in the case of most community foundations; or by the officers or directors of a company in company-sponsored foundations. In a few cases the members of the corporation or trust with power to appoint the trustees or directors are different from or more numerous than the elected trustees. The Northwest Area Foundation is an example of the former and the Southern Education Foundation of the latter. In at least one private foundation, the Trexler Foundation of Allentown, Pennsylvania, the trustees are appointed by the President Judge of the Orphans Court.

In the great majority of foundations, however, boards of trustees are self-perpetuating. This practice has been subject to criticism in certain quarters. To some it represents the perpetuation of power without proper accountability. To others it is the major reason for the lack of diversity among foundation trustees. Yet, it has several practical advantages. It is an uncomplicated procedure. It allows the people who should know best what the board needs for effective functioning to make the choices. It makes possible avoidance of the often abrasive political debate over differences in viewpoint characteristic of public bodies. It emphasizes the importance of trustees being responsible to the trust and its beneficiaries. Alternatives are complex and not altogether satisfactory. They work in a few individual cases, but if the Trexler Foundation practice, for example, were widely adopted, an already overburdened judiciary would be swamped. Self-perpetuation is likely to continue as the normal pattern for foundation boards. The issue, therefore, is how to make it work as well as possible.[3]

The formal machinery for selecting trustees is one thing; the actual practice of many boards is quite another. While the donor is still alive, as noted above, his or her preference is likely to dominate; and in

1. See Ernest V. Hollis: *op. cit.*, pp. 82-6; Waldemar A. Nielsen: *The Big Foundations*, pp. 182-90.

2. George C. Kirstein in *Better Giving*, p. 25, Houghton Mifflin 1975, cites an example of this practice on a hospital board. It probably occurs more frequently than we realize on boards where service is *pro bono publico* and where family feeling is strong. The same impulse that leads to family controlled foundations is at work.

3. See *Trusteeship and the Management of Foundations* by Donald R. Young and Wilbert E. Moore, formerly of the Russell Sage Foundation, for an illuminating discussion of this and related issues. In his essay Moore emphasizes "the potential disadvantages of stuffy conservatism in the face of changing situations" as a result of trustees selecting their successors. Young, on the other hand, is impressed by the many practical advantages of self-perpetuation and finds it preferable to other systems of selection. Pp. 19-20, 50-4.

foundations with a strong family influence new trustees, whether younger members of the family or outsiders, are frequently decided upon in informal family conferences. Sometimes the chairman or a very influential trustee will assume responsibility for recommending additional members, looking upon the selection as virtually his prerogative. In other instances the chairman will ask trustees for the names of suitable candidates who are often elected without further investigation. In all these cases the formality of a board vote is honored, but the choice in fact has been made by one or more individuals—sometimes with exemplary consideration of what the foundation needs, but all too often in a haphazard fashion which gives some justification to the charge of "cronyism."

Whether major decisions are made through informal family discussion or in more formal fashion, foundation boards need to give the most serious thought to the character and quality of their membership. The best ones do, thereby setting an example to others. The most obvious device is the creation of a nominating committee or a committee on trustees, whose responsibility it is to analyze needs, plan for future developments and seek out suitable candidates. This assignment is sometimes assumed by the executive committee, but in general it will be better done by a committee with a single responsibility. Arthur Frantzreb, president of the consulting firm of Frantzreb and Pray Associates, minces no words in emphasizing the importance of this function. "The Committee on Trustees should rank second in importance only to the executive committee. It should define the trustee role and function, prepare and update a trustee profile, maintain lists of and research on trustee candidates (even those who may be elected), continually analyze present strengths of members, design the matching of tasks to people, design procedures for trustee enlistment and programs for trustee education."[4]

What are the qualities most important for the foundation trustee? (1) Interest in and concern for the foundation and its field or fields of operation is certainly one. The job is too demanding for anyone who lacks a fair degree of enthusiasm for the task. (2) Some understanding of the area of the special interest foundation or some broad perspective on the problems of society for the general purpose foundation is essential. Intelligence is assumed, but it needs to be intelligence leavened with sensitivity to people and social problems, with breadth of understanding, and with imagination. (3) Objectivity and impartiality are a *sine qua non*. The board table is no place for special pleading, for temperamental bias, for personal whim. The trustee is judge, not advocate. (4) The board as a whole will need certain special skills among its members— management competence, investment experience or knowledge, familiarity with budgets, knowledge of the law. Not all trustees will possess all these attributes. The value of planning and of Frantzreb's analysis of current members is to make certain that some trustees can contribute

4. "Your Trustee Chairmanship: Its Position and Function" in *Fund Raising Management* for May/June 1975, p. 31.

these services. (5) A capacity for teamwork, for arriving at and accepting a collective decision is highly desirable. Irresolvable differences, the tactics of confrontation, *ad hominem* arguments, lack of respect for one's fellow trustees are destructive of intelligent group decisions. These qualities demonstrate the danger of diversity carried to an extreme, but, as we saw in the last chapter, diversity properly handled can be a constructive force.[5] (6) Finally, a willingness to work is essential. This means a willingness to give time and thought to the affairs of the foundation, to arrange one's personal schedule so as to be available to attend meetings, to serve on committees, to undertake special assignments, to wrestle with the problems of the foundation. Perhaps all these are implicit in an interest in and concern for the foundation cited as the first requisite, but they are important enough to deserve special mention.

The question is sometimes raised whether foundation trustees should be specialists or generalists. Some special kinds of competence are desirable, though in the larger foundations it makes more sense to employ experts on the staff or as consultants. In special purpose foundations specialized knowledge may be either necessary or desirable for some board members. A foundation concerned with the urban problems of Chicago would not be well served by trustees drawn only from farming areas in the Dakotas, and it makes sense to have some doctors or scientists on a foundation concerned with medical research. By and large, however, foundations will be better served by men and women of vision and imagination, people who can bring dispassionate, objective and broadly based judgments to bear on foundation policies and issues. One argument for "men of affairs" (of either sex) on foundation boards is their breadth of view and quick capacity to distinguish the significant from the trivial or irrelevant.[6]

The specifications add up to a difficult, some would say an impossible, assignment. "The trusteeship for great accumulations of money devoted to general purposes presents by no means a simple problem," wrote Henry S. Pritchett in his 1922 Annual Report as president of the Carnegie Corporation. "Such a duty is far more complex than the obligation of trusteeship in the administration of a fund assigned to a specific and definite purpose. To find men of sound judgment, of wide experience, of imagination, of discrimination, who will give time and thought to the duties of trusteeship of this nature has never been easy." If that was true over fifty years ago when there was only a handful of foundations, how much more so today with the proliferation of both foundations and legislation hemming in the actions of trustees and

---

5. Young, *op. cit.,* pp. 44-5, argues for "collegiality" as essential to good board functioning. His arguments will make an instinctive appeal to many trustees who want above all to enjoy quiet and congenial discussions with a minimum of disagreement and rocking of the boat. Enough has already been said about the dangers of too great emphasis on this attitude.

6. See Warren Weaver: *op. cit.,* pp. 105-6. Professor Price of Harvard, referred to in the preceding chapter as dissenting from the view that boards should be more diversified, is clear about the need for liberally trained minds and freedom from special commitments.

making them personally liable for violations. Good and able people have been known to say that they would not dream of serving as a foundation trustee. Others, who are in fact serving, ask where they will find their successors, as legal liabilities and time demands become more serious. This may, indeed, become a problem, though happily there still appear to be public spirited men and women willing to assume both the labor and the risk.

A plan of succession (to revert to the opening paragraph of this chapter), important for all foundations, should provide for both continuity and change. While most charters or founding instruments contain some provision for the selection of successor trustees, that provision is not self-operative or self-realizing. As I talked with trustees across the country, I found that in far too many cases no significant thought had been given to insuring proper succession. Elderly family trustees would admit, when pressed, that they ought to be doing something about their replacements after death, but that they had somehow never got around to doing anything. Is it a reluctance to contemplate the possibility of death, a reluctance which inhibits so many people from drawing up wills? Is it merely procrastination which seems to overtake us as we grow older and less vigorous? Whatever the reason, the result is bad. Common sense suggests that some staggering of ages is desirable, so that not all trustees will reach the end of the road at the same time. And if family or other members have been designated to take over, it would be helpful to break them in under the guidance of senior trustees rather than trusting them to pick up as best they can when death puts them on the spot.

Foundation charters and by-laws can be delightfully vague about length of terms. In some trustees are elected for life; in others, on an annual basis; in a third group terms may be set for a given number of years.[7] Where terms are for one year, re-election is usually automatic—so automatic in fact that the formality of re-election is occasionally dispensed with or overlooked. The intermediate formula of terms of three, five, seven or even ten years has much in its favor, as it is possible to stagger the terms of trustees, which as we shall see below has advantages in introducing change, and which tends to call attention to the need for re-election and planning for the future.

That future should also involve change. Institutions, like people, grow old and become static. What has been called "the iron law of oligarchy" takes over.[8] Those with the greatest interest, energy or ambition collect power around themselves and consciously or unconsciously push aside

---

7. Andrews: *Philanthropic Foundations* 1956, pp. 80-1, gives some amusing examples. "Terms vary from life to a single year, but there is less difference between these extremes than would appear. In the El Pomar Foundation 'the tenure of office of the trustees is indefinite. They remain in office until they die, resign or are removed, whereupon their successors are elected by the remaining members of the Board.' The Twentieth Century Fund limits the terms of its trustees to a single year; re-election, however, is almost certain unless the member himself refuses further service, and in 1954 two members were entering their thirty-third term."

8. See Manser and Cass: *Voluntarism at the Crossroads,* pp. 27-8.

the contributions of others, especially if not supportive of the dominant group's program. As noted in an earlier chapter, it is easier to continue doing what one has done than to introduce change. Institutional renewal, say Manser and Cass, "is potentially a painful process—for someone. It is difficult to explain to a small group of dedicated board members that the program which they have served selflessly for many years must be phased out to give way to new methods of service."

There are two useful devices for facilitating renewal and change. One is to set an arbitrary retirement age. Many foundations do this, but many do not. For Ford Foundation trustees the retirement age is 70; for Rockefeller, 65. During most of its history the Carnegie Corporation had no mandatory retirement age with the result that in earlier years some trustees served until past 80 and one past 90. In 1960 the age limit of 72 was set, and in 1971 this was reduced to 70.[9] Most foundations with mandatory retirement ages seem to favor 65 to 70, but there is no magic in one rather than the other. We all know individuals of 75 who are more youthful in their outlook than their grandchildren, and one should not forget the bitter epitaph, "Died at 30, Buried at 60." If one were inclined to argue the point, much could be said for a later rather than an earlier retirement age; but some cut-off point, hopefully this side of senility, would be an advantage to every board.

The second device is a mandatory limitation on the number of consecutive terms or years of service. This is less common than fixed retirement ages. It faces more resistance, perhaps because it is the more effective of the two in bringing about change. The by-laws of The Ford Foundation permit two successive six-year terms; at the Carnegie Corporation, two four-year terms; at the Edward W. Hazen Foundation, two five-year terms. Again there is no great merit in one coefficient rather than another, but there are two great advantages to the principle of limitation of years of consecutive service. First, it provides the board with a graceful way of saying goodbye to a member who has ceased to make a significant contribution to the work of the foundation. Trustees rarely resign of their own accord unless some new professional or business assignment makes continuation difficult. It is embarrassing to have to explain why the board does not intend to re-elect a member who has served for many years and is devoted to the foundation. With automatic termination, a termination which applies to everyone, no one can feel aggrieved. Second, it provides greater freedom to experiment with younger and different trustees. The board will not be stuck with them for life, but for at most eight or ten or twelve years. In this way new faces, new viewpoints, new sources of ideas can be introduced without a major shift in board composition.

Under this arrangement it is always possible to re-elect to the board a

9. Caryl P. Haskins: "A Foundation Board Looks at Itself" in *Foundation News* for March/April 1972, pp. 9-14. Mr. Haskins was chairman of the trustee committee which recommended this and other changes in the governance of the Carnegie Corporation. His comment on the mandatory age limit was: "This modest further lowering of the age limit seemed consistent with our increased emphasis on rotation and a general desire to involve young men and women in our work." P. 11.

former trustee who has proved to be so invaluable that his services must not be lost. All that is necessary is to allow one year to elapse between termination and re-election. Presumably this will be a rare occurrence, so that no one will have any reason to expect it or be hurt if it does not happen. It could be invoked for family members where family connection is deemed important. Or exceptions to these restrictions could be specified in the by-laws for family members, although the creation of a two-class system of trustees is not desirable. Exception should, of course, be made for the chief executive officer of the foundation if he also serves as a trustee—a practice which appears to find increasing favor. In such a case his service as trustee should continue as long as he remains in his executive position.[10]

The special status of community foundations was noted at the end of the last chapter. They are required by law to have "a representative governing body." The members of that body, it will be recalled, are normally appointed by outside public officials, citizens holding prominent positions in the community (such as the local university president), agencies representing important professional or civic activities (chamber of commerce, bar association and the like), with some designated number nominated by the banks holding the trust funds. Appointments are normally for specific terms, say five or seven years, and not infrequently a member may not succeed himself or may not serve for more than two successive terms.[11] There is, however, room for improvement both in extending these provisions and in planning for new appointments. Outside officials become lax. The practice of suggesting to them "good" appointments may have the practical effect of making distribution committees self-perpetuating. Eugene Struckhoff in the *Handbook* already referred to suggests that community foundation boards should prepare careful analyses of their membership, strengths and weaknesses, duties required, by-laws and other relevant regulations as background for decisions by outside authorities. "The most appropriate conduct by a board seems to be to inform an appointing authority as fully as possible so that he can exercise his function intelligently . . . and, if asked, to suggest several individuals the existing board believes possess those qualities."[12]

10. The Julius Rosenwald Fund limited trustee service to two successive three-year terms (permitting re-election if desirable after the lapse of a year), but made exceptions for the chairman and the president, the former being Mr. Rosenwald and the latter the chief executive officer. See Embree and Waxman: *Investment in People: The Story of the Julius Rosenwald Fund,* Harper and Bros. 1949, Chapter III. The Southern Education Foundation provides that trustees rotated off the board may continue as "members" of the foundation and are urged to attend annual meetings. This provision has been successful in keeping former trustees close to the foundation and in deriving profit from their wisdom and experience.

11. The recently issued regulations for community foundations, while not absolute in their restrictions on membership, have the practical effect of limiting service to not more than ten consecutive years, followed by a period of ineligibility calculated on a special formula. See Treasury Rules and Regulations, Sections 1.170A-9(e)(13)(iv)(A) and (B) and 1.507(a)(8)(ii)(C). The readiness of the Treasury to guard against possible donor and bank control of trustees by such detailed regulations suggests a concern which could easily extend to private foundations, and the private foundations would be wise to take corrective steps.

12. *Op. cit.,* p. VII-17.

It has already been suggested that company-sponsored foundations would do well to add outside members in order to broaden the horizons of corporate philanthropy. Rotation of members, both those from within the company and those reflecting community concerns, would improve the posture and strengthen the performance of corporate foundations. Fresh points of view can lead to enlightened self-interest—to the long term advantage of both company and community.

Both continuity and change are important for the governing boards of foundations. Both can be easily managed *within the foundation* by a little intelligent foresight and planning. The wise donor who establishes his foundation during his life will write in certain restrictions respecting age and length of service—restrictions to which he might himself be an exception. The instrument establishing a foundation by bequest could easily do the same.[13] Exceptions might be made for certain family members, but this becomes awkward and embarrassing in time. It would be much cleaner and simpler to recognize from the start the desirability of providing for constant renewal. For foundations now in existence the trustees have it in their power to add or to amend by-laws which would accomplish this purpose. It is a simple change with significant consequences.

13. The committee of inquiry set up by the National Council of Social Service in England, under the chairmanship of Lord Goodwin, examined these questions. In its report, *Charity Law and Voluntary Organizations,* 1976, the committee concluded: "We recommend (a) that all charities should normally have in their trust instrument a provision for rotation of trustees other than ex officio trustees; (b) that there should be an age limit of 70 for trustees, other than ex officio trustees; (c) that these provisions should apply immediately to new trustees and to existing trustees after three years. . . ."

8 The Dynamics of an Effective Board

"Since ultimate responsibility rests with the trustees, it is of the utmost importance that they become an effective governing body, fully acquainted with the purposes, the past accomplishments, and the potentialities of the organization they direct."

F. EMERSON ANDREWS

THE OBSERVATION THAT the whole is greater than the sum of its parts is true of most social organizations, including governing boards. To be sure, the effectiveness of a board will depend in part on the kind of people who compose it. Intelligent, highly motivated, cooperative individuals with a sense of common purpose will work more effectively together than individualists with limited viewpoints, abrasive personalities and diverse goals. One of the arguments, noted in chapter 6, in favor of the high degree of homogeneity found on most foundation boards is the ability of its members to work harmoniously together with a minimum of disagreement and a maximum sense of common enterprise. Diversity of viewpoint and the regular introduction of fresh perspectives, however, are so important in setting foundation policies that their advantages outweigh their liabilities, especially when experience indicates that diverse boards, properly organized and led, can be highly effective.

In addition to the quality and attitudes of the members, the effectiveness of boards is influenced by a number of factors which deserve careful consideration—more consideration, indeed, than they are frequently given. This chapter will focus on such factors as:

1. Size
2. Physical setting
3. Frequency of meetings
4. Length of meetings
5. Committee structure
6. Role of chairman
7. Role of chief administrative officer
8. Education of trustees
9. Group morale

These belong to what the social scientists call group dynamics, and many studies confirm what experience and common sense reveal to thoughtful observers of group action.[1]

1. Size. The number of trustees may vary from one (an institutional trustee such as a trust company) to 35 (The Minneapolis Foundation). Small family foundations tend to have fewer trustees, say 3-5; large general purpose foundations, to have larger boards. Thus, Ford has 19, Rockefeller 21, Carnegie 17, though The Robert Wood Johnson Foundation has 9 and the Lilly Endowment 8. Most middle-sized and large foundations will have 7 to 12 trustees.[2]

The smaller the board, the greater is likely to be the feeling of unity, of common purpose, of responsibility for the organization, of involvement in its affairs, of participation in its decisions. The larger the board, the greater the input of ideas, the more balanced and judicious the final consensus, the more willing the individual with a minority view to express differing opinions. Since foundations do not have to raise money to meet annual budgets (though community foundations quite properly seek added capital funds) nor operate complex public programs involving people experienced in public relations and community relations (such as the Red Cross, the Boy Scouts, Yale University), they generally do not need the larger boards characteristic of service and educational institutions. No one figure would be right for all. Each foundation board needs to decide on its own optimum size in the light of its situation, program and needs.[3]

2. Physical setting. The atmosphere in which board discussion takes place can have a significant effect on the outcome. Should board meetings be relaxed and informal or should they be strictly businesslike? Too great informality may create the impression that the board's business is not very important. Conversely, highly structured, let's-not-waste-any-time agenda can inhibit discussion, dull the interest and destroy the satisfaction of the participants. Many foundations solve the problem by combining lunch with an afternoon meeting, dinner with an evening meeting, or some similar combination. Others vary the place of meeting, scheduling periodic "retreats" or policy sessions in relaxed locations, often without formal agenda, where leisurely and free-wheeling discussion is encouraged. Even such little things as the shape of the table and the arrangement of chairs make a difference. A

1. I am particularly indebted in this chapter to a review of the findings of the social scientists on group dynamics by Sally Miller Watson.

2. Note, however, that if one divides the number of foundations listed in Edition 4 of *The Foundation Directory* by the number of trustees, the average is 4.2. The smaller number of foundations listed in Edition 5 yields an average of 5.2 trustees per foundation.

3. In 1972 the District Court of Galveston, Texas, ordered an increase in the size of the board of the Moody Foundation from three as specified in the indenture creating the foundation to seven. "After considerable reflection and study in the matter," wrote Judge Godard, "I have concluded that due to the size, function and complexity of the Foundation and for the orderly and efficient operation of same, the Board of Trustees should be expanded so that it could better cope with the demands of today and the future." On appeal, the lower court was reversed, and the foundation, with assets totaling approximately $117 million, is still governed by three trustees.

classroom setting with the chairman (like the teacher) up front is not conducive to the best discussion. Square or rectangular tables where all trustees can readily see and hear each other are more effective than long thin tables. Uncomfortable chairs make people restless; overstuffed chairs tend to make them sleepy. All this is obvious — and often ignored.

3. Frequency of meetings. This varies from never to once a month. Small family foundations feel less need for meetings, since decisions can be easily reached through informal family communication or, as not infrequently happens, trustee action consists in ratifying decisions already made by the donor. Community foundation trustees tend to meet more frequently — sometimes monthly, sometimes every other month. The members of the distribution committee of The Cleveland Foundation meet four times a year plus an annual meeting and serve on one or more of four program committees, each of which meets four or five times a year, and also on administration, finance, nominating and other committees. As a result, each member attends at least twenty meetings per year. For middle-sized and large foundations the norm is probably 3-4 meetings per year. The findings of the Peterson Commission in its scientific sampling of foundations in 1969 give the following table:

	Percentage of Foundations	Percentage of Total Assets
Never	9	1
Once every few years	*	*
Annually	32	6
Biennially[4]	20	20
Quarterly	22	45
Monthly	6	24
Whenever necessary	11	5

*Less than 0.5%

Unless an executive committee, meeting frequently, takes over the responsibilities of the board or unless the board hands over its responsibilities for major decisions to the staff, it is difficult to see how annual meetings can be justified; and there are serious objections to both conditions. The practice of having no board meetings is certainly an evasion of moral responsibility and, when minutes are written up as though there had been meetings, it borders on evasion of legal responsibilities.[5] Semi-annual meetings would seem the minimum

---

4. "Biennially" must be an error for "Semi-annually." The table is to be found in *Foundations, Private Giving, and Public Policy,* p. 249. See Zurcher and Dustan, *The Foundation Administrator,* Appendix I, for additional data on frequency of meetings and size of boards.

5. The *Proceedings of the 7th Biennial Conference on Charitable Foundations,* New York University 1965, carry a summary of a session on "Trustee and Director Involvement and Responsibility" of which Henry Cassorte Smith was moderator. The following comments are pertinent: "Full and accurate minutes of foundation meetings are a necessity from a legal, tax status, and practical standpoint. Needless to add, it is important to have a consistently good attendance of trustees or directors to obtain the benefit of full and varied discussions. Trustees or directors who are absent from a

necessary for even special interest foundations, and three to five meetings per year are desirable depending on the breadth of program interests and the funds available for grants. Operating foundations have different needs, depending on whether the trustees merely set the course and review the operations of the staff or whether they themselves become involved in the program.

4. Length of meetings. In current practice these vary from a few minutes to two or three days.[6] The trustees of The Ford Foundation meet four times a year for two and a half days (Tuesday morning through Thursday lunch with dinner meetings on Tuesday and Wednesday). With travel time for those living away from New York this amounts to four days four times a year. Length, like frequency, will depend on the volume of business, which in turn is a function of amount of money to be spent and breadth of purpose. The examination and approval of recommendations from a committee of experts in a scientific field to which the foundation is restricted take less time than choices among international programs. Review and ratification of the management of the foundation's portfolio by a bank or investment counsel are clearly less demanding than direct management of the foundation's assets by the trustees. Length will also depend on the degree of involvement of trustees in grant decisions. The trustees of one major foundation with assets in excess of $100 million and grants above the $10 million figure meet three times a year for one and a half to two hours per meeting, largely ratifying recommendations of the staff. A small foundation with grants around $350,000 holds two meetings per year extended over an afternoon, evening and the following morning. In this case the staff presents more proposals than can be funded, and the trustees engage in lively and prolonged discussion of their relative merits.

Length and frequency of meetings tend to vary inversely. Where trustees are readily available, as with most community foundations, there is much to be said for frequent meetings. The danger, however, of frequent short meetings is concentration on investment decisions and grant making at the expense of consideration of long range program and policy matters. Some problems need to be talked out at length and in a

---

meeting should promptly be sent complete copies of the minutes. However, it is emphasized that there is no substitute for personal discussion on foundation matters. 'Conference calls,' resumes, etc. cannot possibly serve as a substitute for a face-to-face meeting at which all important problems are fully discussed." Pp. 104-5.

6. The Peterson Commission made a survey of length as well as frequency of board meetings. Here are their findings, *op. cit.,* p. 250:

	Percentage of Foundations	Percentage of Total Assets
Less than 15 minutes	14	*
15-30 minutes	11	1
30 minutes to 1 hour	16	8
1-2 hours	41	30
2-4 hours	14	29
4-6 hours	2	5
6-8 hours	2	1
8 hours or longer	*	25

*Less than 0.5%

leisurely fashion. Each board must decide for itself the optimum combination.

5. Committee structure. For middle-sized and large foundations effectiveness will depend in no small part on the organization of the board so as to make optimum use of the special skills of each member. This applies to boards of sufficient size to justify a committee structure. Most such boards will have an executive committee, a finance or budget or finance and administration committee, one or more program committees, a nominating committee, and sometimes committees on audit, personnel and the like. Special or *ad hoc* committees may be appointed from time to time—e.g., the selection of a new chief officer. Committee structure can occasionally become so elaborate and cumbersome that it defeats its purpose, which is to save the time and energy of the board for central issues of policy and program.

The executive committee is the most important. It is usually small (3-4 members), and since it exercises the powers of the board, it normally consists of senior or prominent trustees. It meets on call or on a regular, usually monthly, schedule between board meetings. It can easily become a powerful, indeed dominating, group within the board as a whole, an inner circle as it were, with the unfortunate result that other trustees come to see themselves as second class citizens and lose interest. It was this concern that led the trustees of the Carnegie Corporation in their 1971 reorganization to abolish the executive committee entirely.[7] Nevertheless, for foundations with only two or three meetings per year, an executive committee is almost indispensable in making grants within board approved programs and dollar limits and in meeting emergency situations of funding and investing. This provides often needed flexibility. In an effective board the executive committee is its servant, not its master.

The creation of one or more program committees depends upon the extent to which the trustees wish to become involved in the distribution of foundation money. In small family foundations, with or without staff, this is normally viewed as a responsibility of the trustees as a whole. We have already noted that in all foundations it is the responsibility of the trustees to set, and from time to time to review, the program objectives. Having done that, some boards are prepared to leave individual grant decisions to the staff with *pro forma* board approval; some accept the recommendations of a program committee which has worked its way through the thicket of grant requests; some assign trustees to one of

---

7. Note Haskins' comments in the article cited in the last chapter: "With a lowered quorum for a meeting of the full board, the placement of nominations in the hands of a new committee for this purpose, and the addition of some administrative responsibilities to those of finance and investment in a revamped committee, it was decided, as indicated earlier, to dispense with an executive committee. In some organizations an executive committee may, over a period of time, become the 'in' group of the board, with a corresponding loss of interest and attention of other trustees. We wished to guard against this, particularly in the light of other recommendations to have more trustees from a wider geographical area and our special concern that the full board be fully and actively involved in the selection and review of the broad substantive programs of the Corporation."

several program committees, each dealing with one major aspect of the foundation's total program. The Cleveland Foundation has four program committees which advise the distribution committee. Trustees of the Charles F. Kettering Foundation serve with staff on task forces dealing with each of the foundation's four fields of concern. Trustees of The Ford Foundation are assigned to committees which work closely with staff in developing programs in each of its seven major areas of activity.

Budget, finance, investment, administrative and similar committees exist to facilitate the necessary housekeeping which is a part of all organizational activity. Foundations with professional staff would do well to leave as much of these duties to the staff as possible, with supervision by an appropriate committee. In any event, they should be relegated to committee consideration in order to free the board as a whole for more important concerns.

6. Role of the chairman. Of all the trustees the chairman[8] plays the central and most significant role. By his example he must lead, persuade and, if necessary, coerce the other trustees into fulfilling their responsibilities. If there are staff, the chairman is the trustee to whom they should most appropriately turn when problems arise, and normally he is the trustee most concerned with the well-being and effectiveness of the staff. His also is the responsibility to make certain that a trustee with special professional competence or experience does not become a self-appointed "expert," limiting the foundation to his or her particular judgments. Trustee skills need to be used, but individual trustees should not be allowed to dominate the board's decisions by claims to knowledge not revealed to other trustees. The chairman must be prepared to give more time and thought to the affairs of the foundation than other trustees.[9]

One word of caution is worth remembering in this connection. The very qualities of leadership and statesmanship so important for the chairman can degenerate into dictatorship. An occasional chairman, just because he is so deeply concerned and involved, assumes more authority than even a chairman should exercise, and it becomes a one man show. The simplest way to guard against this danger, and a good practice even where the danger is believed not to exist, is to limit in the by-laws the chairman's term of office. The Carnegie Corporation, for example, has made it five years. Whatever the term, it will be tempting to extend the tenure of a good chairman for all the obvious reasons of devotion, time, prestige, ability and the like. One buys current ease at the price of future trouble.

7. Role of chief administrative officer. The relations of trustees and staff are the subject of a later chapter. The role of the chief operating

8. The chairman can, of course, be a woman or a man. Fewer women "chair" boards than should in terms of time, interest and ability. I hope that I will be forgiven if I continue to use the generic term "chairman" for the chief presiding officer. "Chairwoman" and "chairperson" do not come trippingly off the tongue.

9. See the Gaither Report on The Ford Foundation, 1949, pp. 127-32, for thoughtful comments on the relation of chairman to board and staff and the role of the executive committee.

head of the foundation is, at least for those foundations with professional staff, one more factor influencing board performance. The selection of the chief administrative officer is the responsibility of the trustees; many would say it is their most important responsibility. The executive director or president must carry out the program and policies laid down by the trustees. By his performance he can make them look good, bad or indifferent. Further, since he is a full-time professional in the field and the trustees are, with notable exceptions, part-time amateurs, he has the opportunity and responsibility for using the trustees to the best advantage, enlisting their interest and support, encouraging them, educating them. It needs to be a relation of mutual trust and confidence if the board is to perform at its best.

8. Education of trustees. An effective board is one that knows its business, understands the issues and can distinguish between the important and the trivial. This is a matter of education. Some men and women seem to be born trustees. Some have it thrust upon them. The majority, however, achieve trusteeship in the full sense of the term by dint of working at the job and educating themselves to its duties. The chairman and the chief administrative officer, either separately or together, can facilitate this process. Between them they should establish the agenda for meetings, making certain that the important issues are up for discussion and that sufficient time is allowed. It is the responsibility of the staff officer to prepare working papers to be sent out in advance of the meeting and to distribute from time to time journals, articles, reprints which will be useful to the trustees. Each officer and board will need to work out the right amount of "homework" for that group of trustees, but a steady flow of careful, accurate information about the foundation's program leavened with thoughtful treatments of broader foundation problems is the secret of an informed, educated and effective board.

9. Group morale. Nothing is so contagious as enthusiasm. Over and above all the other factors affecting a board's performance is the sense of common purpose, of a shared enterprise, the pleasure in serving the welfare of mankind, the satisfaction of a job well done. Board and committee meetings should be looked forward to with pleasure and looked back on with the realization that one comes away richer in insights and ideas. Morale is an elusive quality. When trustees as a group have it, they know it, and they work effectively together for a common cause.

9   To Staff or Not to Staff

"The [Filer] Commission's exhortation to nonprofit organizations to broaden the composition and viewpoints of their boards and staffs won't have great impact on that large group of grant-making organizations which have no staff. The lack of staff is, in some instances, as great an impediment to accessibility as the insularity of governing boards. There can be no real consideration of proposals, much less affirmative outreach, unless there is adequate staff."

FRANCES T. FARENTHOLD

"Trusteeship requires a prejudice against avoidable waste or unnecessary costs of overhead and administration.... And although I suspect that this sensitivity can be easily and unduly exaggerated, it is a sound instinct and one to which endowed philanthropy should pay close attention."

DEAN RUSK

"SOMEBODY MUST SWEAT blood with gift money if its effect is not to do more harm than good," wrote President Henry S. Pritchett of the Carnegie Corporation.[1] That "somebody" must be either the trustees or the staff, and since an enormous amount of hard work is involved, it is surprising—and not a little disturbing—that so few boards of trustees rely on professional staff. In a nation which has elevated managerial skills to a high art, the paucity of such skills in the philanthropic world is the more conspicuous.

The most thorough study of foundation staffing is to be found in *The Foundation Administrator* by Arnold J. Zurcher and Jane Dustan.[2] Using elaborate investigative techniques, the authors could discover in 1970-71

1. Annual Report, 1922, p. 19.

2. Russell Sage Foundation 1972. Zurcher was for many years on the staff of the Alfred P. Sloan Foundation. Jane Dustan is vice president of the Foundation for Child Development.

only 212 foundations employing one or more full-time professional staff and 345 employing full- or part-time professionals. The latter represent less than 1.5% of the foundation universe.[3]

In these foundations, according to Zurcher and Dustan, the maximum number of full-time professional staff was in 1971 1,062 and of full- and part-time 1,411. The full-time professionals were distributed among foundations as follows:

Ford	262	25%
Rockefeller	160	15%
Carnegie		
Commonwealth		
Danforth		
Duke		
Houston		
Kellogg	127	12%
Kettering		
R.K. Mellon		
Mott		
Rockefeller Brothers		
Sloan		

These 13 foundations employed 52% of all full-time professional staff; 48%, or 513, make a very dim Milky Way in the rest of the foundation universe. Ninety percent, as noted in chapter 1, of that universe consists of small family funds with assets of less than $1 million—too small to justify professional staff unless shared with others or unless managed by the donor with or without the assistance of members of his family and business associates. Zurcher and Dustan, however, found 159 foundations with assets of $1-$10 million and 133 foundations with assets ranging from $10 million to $1 billion without any professional staff.

The situation has changed to some extent as a result of the Tax Reform Act of 1969. A survey made among its own members by the Council on Foundations in 1974 revealed a 25% increase in both administrative and "other" employees, including a first professional staff member for 46 out of 350 respondents. Much of this increase is due to the legal and accounting requirements of the 1969 Act. Nevertheless, it remains true that, with the exception of a handful of foundations, the foundation administrator leads a very lonely life, and even for many

3. The Peterson Commission, using a sampling technique in 1969, reached the conclusion that "only one-fifth of all foundations have any paid staff at all, including secretaries. Only 5 percent have any full-time paid staff." *Op. cit.,* p. 87. Even with allowance for the inclusion of clerical as well as professional staff, these figures are probably high. Zurcher and Dustan found only 35 staffed community foundations (or 15% of the total number of such foundations) and 38 staffed company-sponsored foundations (or 0.25% of the 1,500 known company foundations). These figures may be low because they did not investigate foundations with assets under $5 million. James F. Harris and Anne Klepper in their report to the Filer Commission, *Corporate Philanthropic Public Service Activities,* chapter VI, indicate that 45% of company-sponsored foundations have one or more professional staff.

foundations above the $5 million asset level he or she is non-existent.[4]

Is this situation good or bad? Carl Gerstacker, trustee of two foundations each with assets of around $20 million, is proud of the fact that family trustees have taken care of administrative expenses out of their own pockets. "My recommendation, therefore, is for discipline. Government never knows when to stop expanding its services; it has no marketplace to tell it that it has gone too far, as business has. In the same way, foundations often don't know how much to spend on administration. The problem is always where to stop. So keep your administrative expenses and staff to the bare-bones minimum."[5] Those who share this view offer two reasons for their position. The first is the obvious fact that the more money spent for overhead and administration, the less money is available for grants to beneficiaries. The second is the less obvious but nonetheless pertinent observation that, since program and staff go hand in hand, a small staff permits greater flexibility in program. Costs for administration and overhead will naturally run high for operating foundations. While these costs for some purely grant-making foundations seem excessive, the Council's survey of its own members indicates that administrative and overhead costs run around 10%-12% of total expenditures for foundations with assets under $50 million and 6% for those with assets above $50 million.[6]

In deciding on staff there are other considerations besides cost and flexibility. First of all comes the question of efficiency. Potential beneficiaries of a foundation have a right to present their petitions. Someone should see them or answer their letters. Requests need to be investigated. Proposals need to be winnowed. Grants need to be followed up both to insure that the money is being properly spent and to learn from past decisions how to serve the public welfare better in future choices. Increasingly complex accounting is required by the Tax Reform Act of 1969. Forms must be filed and, as will be argued in chapter 12, reports need to be prepared and distributed. To economize on staff may be a case of being penny wise and pound foolish. "Such economy in personnel is unwise where substantial grants are involved," writes Emerson Andrews. "Giving away money effectively is a complicated business. The efficiency of a foundation is measured by the benefits resulting from its grants, not by the number of dollars given or a low mathematical ratio between administration costs and disbursements."[7] A low cost grant because ill thought out or inadequately investigated may prove to be a high cost waste of foundation money. The need for staff

4. See the Council's *Report and Recommendations*, 1975, pp. III 5-9. The Zurcher and Dustan analysis is to be found in chapter 1 of their excellent book.

5. "Let 'Outsiders' Control Family Foundation Boards" in *Foundation News*, September/October 1975, p. 18.

6. See Zurcher and Dustan: *op. cit.*, Appendix I. For the Council's data see their *Report and Recommendations*, p. III-8 and Tables 1 and 2 in the Appendix. A recent illuminating analysis of the range of administrative costs by type of program as well as by asset size is to be found in the article by Sally Miller, "Administrative Costs: How and Why They Differ" in *Foundation News*, November/December 1975.

7. *Philanthropic Foundations*, p. 129.

will vary with the nature of the foundation. The larger and more general the purposes, the greater the need for professional help; but all foundations, save those with trustees who virtually make a career of managing them, would improve their operations with staff assistance. Too many which could well afford such help are limping along without it.[8]

The first quotation at the head of this chapter presents a second argument for staffing. If foundations are private money committed to the public good, what responsibilities have the trustees to insure that the foundation is both visible and available? The secrecy with which many foundations have carried on their philanthropic work has not only militated against their effectiveness, but has also been unfair to potential recipients. This is one of the complaints of the Donee Group to whom reference has been made in earlier chapters, and the complaint is not without justification. "The Donee Group recommends that there be a legal requirement that any organization making grants in excess of $100,000 per year employ at least one full-time professional (i.e., not a bookkeeper, accountant or donor's secretary) or, as an alternative, join in a cooperative venture with other organizations sharing common staff."[9] One can question the wisdom of a legal requirement and even the minimum of $100,000 while agreeing with the central thrust of their argument that good foundation practice requires both accessibility and positive outreach into the areas of the foundation's concerns. "The worst pitfall," according to Nicholas Kelley, former trustee of the Carnegie Corporation, "is to waste money, to make a grant because somebody appears with a pretty good case and you do not think of anything very much better to do. It is too easy for those things to multiply."[10]

Closely related to this concept of the role of the foundation is the contribution which professional staff can and do make to the agencies supported by the foundation and to many of those whose requests are declined. Their personal concern and professional help will often be more valuable than the grant itself. While care must be observed not to interfere with or dictate to requesting organizations, many need help with their internal operations or their proposed budget. Some need assistance in rewriting their proposals. Others need guidance in where to turn for support. Staff members of the larger community foundations, such as The Cleveland Foundation, are making an important contribution in these ways, but even a small family foundation, such as the Dyer-Ives Foundation in Grand Rapids with assets of around $150,000 and

8. Note the comment of Zurcher and Dustan, *op. cit.,* p. 129: "With no one to tend store, many foundations have been unable to discharge even the most elementary administrative responsibilities. In far too many cases, there has been no one to establish operating standards that would pass muster with the most indulgent student of administration; no one to compile, write, and distribute a public report; no one to provide the hard data about the foundation for appropriate reference volumes or for those making legitimate inquiry. Optimists on staffing believe that these weaknesses have become so obvious that they can no longer be ignored."

9. *Op. cit.,* p. 21.

10. *Proceedings of 2nd Biennial Conference on Charitable Foundations,* New York University 1955, p. 219.

annual grants between $25,000 and $30,000, has part-time professional staff for the explicit purpose of counseling agencies seeking funds and advising them where to apply for assistance. Most staffed foundations give far more than money, and staff initiative in seeking out and developing community programs can be an important factor in foundation effectiveness.

The cost of a full-time administrator together with the expenses of office and overhead for a foundation with an annual grant budget of $100,000, as proposed by the Donee Group, would be excessive unless the foundation has its own operating program or makes through its staff a significant human and professional contribution to the community it serves. There are, however, other solutions to this problem. Part-time staff is one. Sharing staff by two or more foundations is another. Technical advisers and consultants on a fee basis, widely used by the larger foundations to supplement permanent staff, provide the possibility of cost saving to smaller foundations.[11] Slowly at first but more rapidly in the last ten years associations of foundations—regional, state and local—are developing with services of value to all members. Community foundations, as already noted, are in a strategic position to provide professional assistance to unstaffed foundations within their orbit. With the recent increase in legal and accounting requirements, managerial agencies are beginning to appear, providing both technical and general assistance on a contract basis. In short, there are ways of making foundation operations more effective and therefore more valuable to society without unreasonable overhead costs. They need to be used.

Good administrators are no easier to find in the foundation field than in any other. Indeed, the task may be harder. There are as yet too few of them to constitute a profession. There is no professional association. There are no professional training programs. There is no dearth of applicants, for plenty of people think it would be a pleasant occupation to give away other people's money. The occupational hazards of the job are the insidious growth of attitudes of omniscience and omnipotence, and staff can degenerate in time to becoming office holders without imagination.

Administrative competence and professional knowledge combined with imagination, integrity and humility are what every foundation needs. They will be found in the most unsuspected places, provided one really looks for them and avoids the temptation to staff foundations, as too often happens with company-sponsored foundations, with individuals who have not quite made the grade in the main line.

The role of the chief administrative officer is a complex one. Subject to policies determined by the trustees, he should run the show, setting up the administrative machinery, selecting additional staff if necessary, preparing the budget and controlling expenditures. Either alone or in

---

11. Frederick P. Keppel, one of the great presidents of the Carnegie Corporation, used to say that he preferred to "buy his milk than keep a cow." Quoted in Andrews: *Philanthropic Foundations*, p. 131.

conjunction with his colleagues, if any, he must review and investigate requests for grants and prepare recommendations for trustee action. In many situations he can play a catalytic role in the development of new programs. He must keep the trustees informed and should help them to understand better their role and function. He is the agent of the board and has the responsibility for carrying out the program and policies approved by the trustees.

Conversely, trustees have certain responsibilities in relation to staff. The central and most important of these is to make sure that the foundation is being managed in accordance with the goals and policies adopted by the trustees. There must be no confusion as to what those policies are and no equivocation regarding their execution. Are inquiries being sympathetically answered? Is help being offered to those in need of advice? Are financial records properly kept? Is the "housekeeping" efficient? Are necessary forms filed?

One of the difficult problems in foundation management is project evaluation. The success or failure of grants provides lessons for the future. Monitoring programs is time consuming work, and in that fact lies one of the arguments for professional staff. Thoughtful observers of the foundation scene report a widespread, some even say shocking, lack of information on this score.[12] The "expenditure responsibility" for certain types of grants under the Tax Reform Act of 1969 and the temper of Congressional questioning of foundation programs which led up to the Act have stimulated greater attention to project evaluation. Program appraisals take time and money. While the requirement of reports from recipients and the use of consultants can reduce the cost, staffed foundations are clearly in a better position than trustee managed foundations to follow through.[13] When they do, it is important for staff to communicate the evaluations, especially when negative, to the trustees. Since trustees make the final decisions, they need to know the results. "However, to be fully effective," writes Bolman, executive director of the Exxon Education Foundation, "a foundation must build evaluation into every program and project from their inception, and it must be prepared to apply a substantial portion of its resources to this evaluation. If it is conceded that the aim of a foundation is to achieve a set of objectives and

12. See the Peterson Commission Report, chapter 10 and appendix IV, tables A.45, A.46 and A.47. Yorke Allen, Jr., of the Rockefeller Brothers Fund in an unpublished paper, February 1975, and others have expressed concern. Zurcher and Dustan in *The Foundation Administrator*, p. 111, note that "lack of evaluation procedure for completed projects" is listed by 30% of foundation administrators as one of the frustrations of their job, the highest listing of 16 items mentioned.

13. For discussion of the do's and don'ts, the ways and means, of project evaluation see Orville G. Brim, Jr.: "Do We Know Where We Are Going?" in Fritz Heimann (ed.); *The Future of Foundations,* Prentice-Hall 1973; Merrimon Cuninggim: *Private Money and Public Service,* McGraw-Hill Book Co. 1972, pp. 120-2; Yorke Allen, Jr.: "Evaluating Foundations" already referred to; Stephen White: *Evaluation of Foundation Activities,* Sloan Foundation 1970; Milton T. Bratz: "Maurice Falk Medical Fund Project Evaluation Program" 1974; the Evaluation Plan of the Irwin-Sweeney-Miller Foundation (mimeographed) 1974; Frederick deW. Bolman: "Towards Greater Effectiveness," the 1972-73 annual report of the Exxon Education Foundation; William G. Wing: "It's Easier Said Than Done But Some Foundations Do Try" in *Foundation News* for November/December 1973, pp. 42-8.

not just to give away money, it is clear that such rigorous evaluation is not a diversion of funds and efforts from a foundation's main purpose, but central to that purpose."[14]

Trustees also have the responsibility for providing satisfactory conditions of employment—adequate office space, salaries commensurate with responsibilities, fringe benefits, reasonable security, formally adopted retirement and vacation policies. More than these, however, trustees should make sure that professional staff have a chance to grow and to refresh themselves. In all but a handful of large foundations the job of the administrator is likely to be a lonely one. We have seen that, in most foundations with staff, the staff consists of one individual, either part-time or full-time. He or she will be working for the most part under considerable pressure—from those wanting money on one side and on the other from the need to provide to the trustees the help they need and expect. The very isolation of the job makes the sympathetic encouragement of trustees that much more important. Leaves of absence, freedom for outside activities, encouragement to pursue one's professional career and writing—all these help to keep staff alive and growing and thereby improve the operations of the foundation.

It is essential that both trustees and staff understand their respective roles and responsibilities. It has been alleged that some boards of trustees have become the captives of a powerful palace guard. If so, this is an inversion of authority which rests first and always with the trustees. They may, indeed they should, delegate responsibility for the administration of the foundation. Their role is to set policy, not to manage. They may, and many foundations with competent staff do, delegate responsibility for making grants up to some designated size or within some designated total amount; but in doing so they must decide those limits and establish procedures for reviewing what the chief administrator has done. McGeorge Bundy, president of The Ford Foundation, lays down three principles determining the trustees' relation to the operating head:

> "First, trustees should never keep a chief executive officer beyond the point when they are persuaded that they can do better with someone else; second, trustees, even of very large, complex, and professionalized foundations, should not delegate, even to the most trusted of presidents, their final responsibility for program choice; and third, even when—as they often should—they delegate wide direction in execution and give great weight to professional recommendations, trustees should make the fullest possible use, both formally and informally, of the power of constitutional monarchs elsewhere: to be informed, to advise, to warn—and I would add the quite different power to forbid."[15]

14. Exxon Education Foundation 1972-73 Annual Report, pp. 7-8.

15. "Foundation Trustees: Their Moral and Social Responsibilities," published by The Ford Foundation, 1975.

Conversely, trustees should support their staff. They should try to appoint a chief administrator who could appropriately serve as a member of the board of trustees. They will be ill served if they select someone who can be treated as an errand boy. While the power of decision is unquestionably theirs, trustees should set themselves procedures to be followed in approving grants. Obviously they should not ride their own hobbies, but they also should not allow themselves to be used to support the concerns of others. The seeker of funds, unless quite sophisticated, will sometimes try an end run, thinking to get a trustee to do battle in his favor at the next board meeting. Such side door antics are demoralizing to a professional staff and disastrous to a well thought out foundation program. Sometimes staff members will need to carry on a long series of negotiations with a potential recipient before the proposal is in shape to be presented to the trustees. There should be sufficient trust and understanding between trustees and staff to permit the latter to proceed with confidence that the trustees will not jerk the rug out from under them. The wise foundation administrator will make it quite clear that the final decision rests with the trustees; but too many turndowns after long buildups of expectation will destroy the effectiveness of staff and the reputation of the foundation.

Logic and experience point to the need for better foundation management than has been the norm. Indeed, it can be argued that an increase in the number of foundations with professional staff and the consequent improvement in their programs are necessary for the survival of foundations as a system of philanthropy. Why is there such reluctance? Zurcher and Dustan suggest a number of reasons in chapter 1 of their study. Since most foundations began as small institutional conduits for family philanthropy, they had no need for professional help, and the amateur approach had become a habit by the time the foundation had outgrown its early stages. Often the donor was convinced—and sometimes the results justified the belief—that he could be more imaginative and constructive than professional philanthropoids. His successors have often felt not only that they could carry on his interests more faithfully than outsiders hired to do a job, but also that they should remain true to his method of reaching decisions. In many charitable trusts the donor so limited the freedom of his trustees that few significant decisions needed to be made. And in some foundations, especially those established as trusts, handsome fees to the trustees could hardly be justified if professional staff were employed to do the work.

Allowance must be made for the small foundation managed by trustees who devote a substantial amount of time and attention to its affairs. The commitment and concern of these individuals are invaluable and go far toward removing the need for paid staff. No doubt all the factors mentioned by Zurcher and Dustan have influenced the middle-sized and large foundations without staff, but they do not completely account for the present unsatisfactory situation. The central reason is the failure of trustees to recognize their responsibility for meeting public needs with a carefully planned program of philanthropy, constantly reviewed in the light of changes in the social, economic and political

70

order of society, and occasionally revised. And so we come full circle. To do the constructive and creative job which society is demanding of foundations, most trustees need the help of professional staff. In order to be persuaded to add staff, trustees need a broader vision of their role in society.

10 Compensation of Trustees

"Payment for the oversight of philanthropic activities is not in the American tradition. The trustees of educational institutions ranging from the public schools to universities and of health and welfare agencies traditionally receive no compensation. Yet the oversight of such institutions and agencies commonly requires more time and effort than does the management of a foundation, for the reason that a foundation is less likely to conduct an extensive operating program. However, it is in the American tradition to compensate trustees of trust funds, and this may have led to the payment of the trustees of a few foundations organized as trusts."

DONALD R. YOUNG

YOUNG'S STATEMENT IS both accurate and misleading.[1] In percentage terms it is correct. At the time of the 1969 Hearings in Congress on the Tax Reform Act, F. Emerson Andrews conducted an unpublished survey of foundation practice regarding fees to trustees. Using a 5% random sample, he reviewed returns from 1,000 foundations, 978 of which, or 98%, paid no compensation for trustee service.[2] On the other hand, Zurcher and Dustan in their survey of foundations with professional staff found 119 foundations whose trustees received compensation, and the most recent (1976) survey by the Council on Foundations of its own membership revealed 67 members providing fees to trustees.[3]

1. See *Trusteeship and the Management of Foundations*, p. 41.

2. A comparison of Andrews' figures with the distribution of foundations by size in chapter 1 indicates a high degree of accuracy in the random sample:

	Andrews		Foundation Directory	
Over $10 million	16	1.6%	449	1.8%
$1-$10 million	85	8.5%	2,055	8.2%
Under $1 million	899	89.9%	22,421	89.9%

3. The 119 foundations in the Zurcher and Dustan survey constituted 22% of the 540 foundations on which they obtained data regarding fees. The Council's 67 members compose 27.5% of the 243 which responded. Both surveys contained a disproportionate number of larger foundations.

No exhaustive survey has ever been made to determine how many foundations provide compensation to their trustees; but the figures cited, which are admittedly incomplete, suggest that the number is not insignificant. Two percent, to take Andrews' figure, of 26,000 foundations is 520. We do know that foundations set up as charitable trusts are more likely to provide fees to trustees than foundations established as corporations; and there is some evidence that the practice of paying fees is on the increase.

What are the arguments pro and con? The arguments against payment of compensation to trustees for their service as trustees can be simply stated. (1) It reduces the amount of money available to the beneficiaries of the foundation. (2) It is incompatible with the American tradition that being a trustee of a nonprofit organization is an important form of public service. (3) It treads close to the dangerous quicksand of self-service. While not prohibited by law, the payment of honoraria to trustees of nonprofit organizations is viewed with the same suspicion and skepticism by the general public as the payment of large salaries. (4) As Young points out, the trustees of colleges and universities, hospitals and museums, welfare agencies and community organizations, do not receive compensation. They are responsible for more complex operating programs than the trustees of most foundations. It seems somewhat anomalous to pay foundation trustees.

There are, however, two sides to the issue. (1) It is the thesis of this study that foundation trustees carry an important and heavy set of responsibilities. If banks, investment counselors and lawyers are to be paid for their services to the foundation in safeguarding funds, why should not trustees be paid for their work both in managing income and in distributing grants? (2) The Tax Reform Act of 1969 has complicated the life of foundation trustees, requiring additional care on their part and subjecting them to additional penalties for failure. They deserve some reward for their pains and may need some inducement to serve. (3) Furthermore, service as a trustee is, or should be, time consuming. This obviously varies with the number and length of meetings, committee service and pre-meeting preparation. For many trustees the combination constitutes a serious lien on their time. The presence of staff members can lighten this load, though this does not always follow. Most foundations, however, as we saw in the last chapter, are trustee managed. (4) With diversification of board composition, compensation may become an important consideration in accepting membership. The trustee described by Lindeman[4] could afford to donate his time. The new trustees resulting from the democratization of boards may not be able to donate their time and service as easily. It was this consideration which led the trustees of the Carnegie Corporation recently to institute a $250 per meeting honorarium for all trustees. (5) Annual retainers, rather than fees for attending meetings, serve the same purpose as well as applying a certain amount of moral pressure on trustees to do their homework. To accept a fee is to feel under obligation. (6) Directors' fees

4. See chapter 6, p. 40.

in the business world are increasing in size as the responsibilities of directors increase. While the parallel is not exact, there is a tendency for the practices of the nonprofit world to follow those of the business world.

It would seem reasonable to assume that the larger and wealthier foundations with the heavier work load would be more likely to pay fees to trustees. On the other hand, Zurcher and Dustan maintain just the reverse, "namely, that compensation to trustees may rise to fairly generous levels—if there is any compensation at all—in foundations without staff and declines markedly as foundations take on staff."[5] The data provided by the 1976 Council survey of its members, while incomplete, give probably as accurate a distribution by size as is available. The figures in parentheses indicate the number of foundations with full- or part-time staff. It will be noted that, with the exception of the $25-$100 million class where the results may be skewed by the small number of respondents, there is an increase in the percentage of foundations providing compensation as the foundations increase in size.

Assets in $ millions	Pay Fees to Board Members			
	Yes		No	
	No.	Pct.	No.	Pct.
Under $1	8(3)	17%	40	83%
$1-$5	16(11)	22	57	78
$5-$10	12(10)	33	24	67
$10-$25	12(11)	36	21	64
$25-$100	6(6)	21	22	79
$100 Up	13(13)	52	12	48
	67(54)	28%	176	72%

The range of trustee compensation is very great, but for most foundations the amounts are quite modest. Many foundations pay a fee from $25 to $250 per meeting. Others pay an annual "retainer" ranging from $100 to $10,000. Ford and Andrew W. Mellon Foundations, for example, pay $5,000 (with more for service on various committees), Robert Wood Johnson $4,000, Rockefeller Foundation $3,000. The Fleischmann Foundation, which prides itself on being completely trustee managed, provides fees of $10,000 to each of its five trustees (with additional compensation to the chairman, who serves as chief administrative officer.)[6]

5. *Op. cit.,* p. 101. This is of course true in absolute numbers because the number of staffed foundations, as we found, is relatively small. In percentage terms the picture is quite different.

6. In 1972 the trustees of The Moody Foundation petitioned Judge Godard of the District Court of Galveston, Texas, for permission to receive compensation of $10,000 each. The original trust indenture of 1942 prohibited the payment of compensation to the trustees. Judge Godard found that since the original indenture "matters for which Trustees must be responsible have increased in number and complexity. It is not practical or expedient from the standpoint of The Moody Foundation to provide no compensation for a trustee's services as such." Accordingly the judge amended the original indenture to allow for fees and approved the recommendations of the trustees that compensation be set at $10,000 per trustee.

Mention was made at the beginning of the chapter that foundations established as trusts are more likely to pay fees than those which are incorporated. This is probably due to the fact that charitable trusts have tended to follow the practice of private trusts in compensating trustees — a practice which has been encouraged by the frequent designation of a bank or trust company as either sole trustee or as one trustee along with two or three individuals. Since the bank expects to be paid for its services, individual trustees are inclined to expect compensation for theirs.

State laws governing the payment of fees to trustees vary from state to state and may also invite expectations on the part of trustees. In New York State, for example, the Surrogate's Court Procedure Act, sections 2308 and 2309, set the limits. In essence the Act provides for fees equal to 7% of the first $2,000 of income and 5% of the balance of income. Where the annual income amounts to $4,000 or more and where there is more than one trustee, a second trustee is entitled to the same amount as a sole trustee; if there are more than two trustees, the fees to which two trustees are entitled must be apportioned among the trustees in accordance with their respective services. This is true of all charitable trusts created after April 1, 1948. For those established prior to that date the second and third trustees are entitled to the same amount as a sole trustee, but if there are more than three, the compensation to which the three are entitled must be apportioned among all of them according to their respective services. The trust instrument may specify lower or higher fees, in which case its stipulation takes precedence over the terms of the Surrogate's Court Procedure Act.

There are some fees, however, which without further explanation are difficult to justify. James Duke specified in the trust instrument establishing The Duke Endowment that the 15 trustees should receive as compensation for their work equal shares of 3% of the income of the endowment. In the last year reported this amounted to $49,660 per trustee (Doris Duke declining to accept her share). The trustees meet ten times per year and dispense over $19 million. They have investment and other responsibilities, including committee assignments. The sizable fees are mandated by the terms of the indenture and could not be reduced without court action upsetting Mr. Duke's stipulation. Indeed, they are less than the trust law of New York State, where The Duke Endowment is located, would permit. But are such large sums necessary or desirable as honoraria to individuals who have other occupations and for whom service to the Endowment is part-time?

In a number of other cases, whether or not the donor has stipulated the amount, trustees of charitable trusts have been receiving substantial fees. For example, a review of 990 forms on file in The Foundation Center for large and middle-sized New York charitable trusts discloses the following payments, all presumably legal under the Surrogate's Court Procedure Act: The Dula Education Foundation according to its 1974 return paid a total of $82,997 in fees to three individuals and a bank; the Louis Calder Foundation reported in its 1974 return payments of $125,000 to each of three individual trustees. In the same year the Seth Sprague Educational and Charitable Foundation indicated payments of

$47,839 to each of four trustees, one being a bank. The Statler Foundation in 1973 paid each of three individual trustees $34,187. The Mary Flagler Cary Charitable Trust, established in 1968 and with reported assets in 1973 of $72,500,000, paid in 1973 the handsome sum of $216,133 to each of its four individual trustees. In 1975 the total for four trustees was scaled down to $368,367.

It is not uncommon for banks to receive larger fees—again perfectly legal—in payment for their investment and custodial services. And many individual trustees, especially when serving as officers of the foundation, spend substantial amounts of their time managing its affairs. This may account for some of the figures above. It is very difficult, indeed often impossible, to extract from the 990 forms information about fees for service as trustees as distinct from fees for professional and other services.

Reason would suggest that the amount of compensation for trustees should be related to the amount of time and work involved—the number and length of meetings, committee requirements, the presence or absence of staff to carry on day-to-day management—and it ought to bear some justifiable relation to the size of the foundation, the nature and complexity of its holdings, the scope of its programs and the annual volume of grants. There would seem to be no justification for the performance of a Massachusetts foundation, now no longer in existence, which only a few years ago had assets of just under $2 million, made three grants amounting to $35,000, and paid its four trustees a total of $30,186 in fees.

A case can be made for providing a measure of compensation to foundation trustees, but our long and honorable tradition of voluntary, unpaid, charitable service should not be discarded lightly. Schools, colleges, universities, hospitals, orchestras, museums and the host of social service agencies could not function without the donated services of public spirited citizens. It will be a sorry day when the directors and trustees of these organizations expect and receive compensation for their services. Should foundation trustees expect more? If so, it is perhaps only because the 1969 Tax Reform Act makes them so much more closely accountable and places them under much greater potential sanctions.

If fees are to be paid, serious thought needs to be given to their size, both in absolute and in relative terms. What is reasonable is a matter of judgment. In the light of the American tradition of voluntarism and of the 1969 Tax Reform Act prohibition against excessive compensation, it seems difficult to justify fees to trustees *as trustees* of more than $5,000-$15,000. For foundations with assets of $1-$10 million and grant programs ranging from $100,000 to $500,000 compensation to trustees in excess of 3%-5% of grants should be examined carefully and justified by special circumstances and special demands. For foundations with assets above $10 million the ratio of fees to grant programs should decrease rapidly. For the very large foundations they should be, and indeed they are, a minute fraction. Total compensation at Mellon, Carnegie and Robert Wood Johnson run under 0.2% of grant programs, at Ford around 0.05%.

There is no moral justification, whatever the law permits, for diverting more than a very modest sum from the proper beneficiaries of a foundation to the pockets of the trustees who are responsible for the charitable trust. Those who reject this position would do well to reflect on the ammunition that large payments to trustees can easily provide for the next populist attack on the foundations.

11   1969 and All That

"A trustee of a foundation, whether established by an agreement of trust, created under federal law, or incorporated under the state law, has certain duties and responsibilities which are clearly defined by law and established rules for the conduct of trustees. These duties encompass a wide area of responsibility."

ROBERT H. MULREANY

"Many forms of conduct permissible in a workaday world for those acting at arm's length, are forbidden by those bound by fiduciary ties. A trustee is held to something stricter than the morals of the market place. Not honesty alone, but the punctilio of an honor the most sensitive, is then the standard of behavior. As to this there has developed a tradition that is unbending and inveterate."

JUDGE CARDOZO

THIS STUDY IS primarily concerned with those broad responsibilities which trustees must accept if foundations are to fulfill their purpose of serving the public good. Some of those responsibilities are rooted in law, both common and statutory. The law of trusts, for example, has a long history and constitutes a well defined body of law. The laws governing charitable corporations, however, while varying from state to state, permit somewhat greater latitude. Implicit in the fiduciary relationship are other responsibilities which, although not explicitly defined by statute, are implicit in the concept of trusteeship and are being more widely recognized and enforced in judicial proceedings. "The fiduciary relationship," writes Marion R. Fremont-Smith, "arises in many different situations, and although it is considered to be most intense in the trust, directors and officers of corporations are also fiduciaries. Their legal duties have been developed from the same principles as those applicable to trustees."[1]

---

1. *Foundations and Government,* Russell Sage Foundation, 1965, p. 134. Throughout this chapter I am indebted to this excellent and comprehensive treatment of the subject. See also Myles L. Mace, "Standards of care for trustees" in *Harvard Business Review,* January/February 1976.

States as well as the federal government have substantial responsibilities for the supervision of foundations, whether in the form of trusts or of corporations. Depending on state law, the attorney general, as the representative of the sovereign and the guardian of the rights and interests of the public, possesses with respect to foundations a variety of statutory or common law remedial powers. State probate courts and courts of equity may also play a supervisory role.

In recent years federal tax legislation and Treasury regulations affecting foundations have substantially increased. The 1954 Tax Act provided broad rules for charitable organizations—the famous 501(c)(3) classification—covering investment, payout, excessive compensation and other matters and set penalties of loss of tax-exemption for violations. These were materially strengthened and extended in the Tax Reform Act of 1969. It established a category called "private foundations," and for the first time spelled out a series of penalty taxes, supplementing the threat of loss of tax-exemption, to be levied primarily on private foundations or their managers. The 1969 Act also included various provisions encouraging greater supervision of private foundations by the states, which had admittedly been lax in their supervision.[2] Some of the private foundation rules were modified slightly by the Tax Reform Act of 1969.

In 1975 the Office of Assistant Commissioner for Employee Plans and Exempt Organizations was established by statute. It provided for the first time a vertically integrated structure within the Internal Revenue Service and a senior IRS official responsible for supervision of exempt organizations, including foundations and other charities.

What this all adds up to is the uncomfortable fact that foundation trustees must function in an increasingly tangled web of rules and regulations. These were in part due to the abuses engaged in by a few unscrupulous trustees—abuses which invited legislative correction or, as so often happens, over-correction. But they are also the inevitable consequence of an increasingly complex society dominated more and more by a bureaucracy of forms and computers. In any event, it is essential that the foundation trustee know not only what he ought to do, but also what he may and may not do. Any detailed discussion of the latter properly belongs in the domain of the lawyers. This chapter is a layman's version of the major legal as well as moral duties of the foundation trustee, with particular concern for the trustees of private foundations.

1. The duty of loyalty to the beneficiary is the absolute basis on which all trust arrangements depend. "Administration of the trust solely in the interest of the public is the *sine qua non* against which the foundation trustee's loyalty, his most fundamental duty owed the public, must be tested."[3] Loyalty to the beneficiary requires the avoidance of

2. See Marion R. Fremont-Smith: "Impact of the Tax Reform Act of 1969 on State Supervision of Charities" in *Harvard Journal On Legislation*, Vol. 8, pp. 537-69.

3. Mulreany: *op. cit.*, p. 1066. Note also Fremont-Smith's statement, *op. cit.*, p. 94: "A trustee's interest must always yield to that of the beneficiary. The fact that a trustee acted in good faith in a transaction where there was a question of self-dealing or self-interest is not an adequate defense to a charge of violation of the duty of loyalty;

anything approaching an act of self-dealing in financial matters, the avoidance of conflicts of interest in grant making, and the assurance of the distribution of all possible funds to the beneficiaries.

The Internal Revenue Code of 1954 had permitted "arm's length" transactions between a foundation and persons closely related to it, a provision which led to some of the abuses uncovered by Representative Patman. Section 4941 of the Internal Revenue Code laid down strict prohibition against acts of self-dealing which covered a wide range of financial transactions involving the foundation and "disqualified persons." The latter include "foundation managers" (trustees, directors, officers and those with similar responsibilities), substantial contributors (and certain relatives of substantial contributors), government officials plus others with designated amounts of financial interest in businesses related in certain ways to the foundation. Exception is allowed for reasonable compensation for services rendered by disqualified persons, such as salaries to staff members and fees to trustees.[4] To avoid the risk of penalty taxes through inadvertent violation of the self-dealing regulations, every foundation should maintain on record a complete list of all disqualified persons. A further safeguard to officers and trustees is to obtain written professional advice that the action contemplated is legitimate, in which case even a later finding that the action was an improper investment or a taxable expenditure should relieve the officer or trustee from the penalty tax.[5]

Conflict of interest in awarding grants has long been a delicate issue. It is the rare foundation trustee who does not serve on one or more *pro bono publico* boards or committees or whose wife or husband or children do not serve. Disappointed petitioners and people hostile to the "power" they believe foundations wield are quick to suspect favoritism or undue influence when they see the trustee of the granting foundation also serving on the board of the recipient agency. In drawing up their "code of conduct" the trustees of the Northwest Area Foundation addressed themselves squarely to this issue. "Private foundations must strive so far as possible to be above suspicion. It is not enough that the Directors and the Staff *believe* that they are operating from the highest motives, and that any particular action is innocent, regardless of its appearance. So far as possible, actions and relationships must avoid an appearance of impropriety which raises questions in the minds of the public."

The Northwest Area Foundation and a handful of others have adopted, mostly within the past decade, written guidelines or codes of conduct for trustees or staff or both. Full disclosure of all outside affiliations is the

---

neither is ignorance nor innocence. It is immaterial whether the beneficiary is damaged."

4. See Donald E. Vacin: "Guidelines for Foundation Administration under the Tax Reform Act" in *Taxes* for May 1974, and Alvin J. Geske: "Indirect Self-Dealing and Foundation's Transfers for the Use or Benefit of Disqualified Persons" in *Houston Law Review* for January 1975, for detailed expositions of a complicated set of prohibitions.

5. See Norman Sugarman: "Penalties on Foundations and Foundation Managers: How to Avoid Them" in *Proceedings of the Eleventh Biennial Conference on Charitable Foundations,* New York University, 1973, pp. 235-57.

most common recommendation. Ford, Rockefeller, Cleveland and North-west, for example, require annually updated rosters of such connections. The Chicago Community Trust and Northwest require relevant business affiliations as well as nonprofit ties. Some stipulate that trustees with potential conflicts of interest shall not vote on the issue; others insist that such trustees shall absent themselves from the board discussion as well as at the final vote. The Charles Stewart Mott Foundation goes even further, recommending that "Foundation personnel (Trustees, officers, and staff) should generally not be associated in a controlling capacity such as a Board member or officer if this puts the person or a combination of Foundation-related persons in a dominant role, or as an employee, with any prospective or present grantee or recipient of an appropriation of the Foundation."[6]

Loyalty to the beneficiaries entails maximizing the funds available for the foundation's charitable purposes. In 1950 Congress passed a tax law which for the first time prohibited "unreasonable" accumulations of income. The Danforth Foundation was one of the few foundations to be penalized under the permissive terms of section 504.[7] Other foundations, such as the Lilly Endowment, with major holdings in high growth and low yield stocks, while not accumulating income, maintained a relatively low rate of pay-out in relation to market value of assets.[8] Section 4942 of the Internal Revenue Code now stipulates that foundations shall pay out whichever is the higher of their adjusted net income or a minimum investment return represented by a given percent of investment assets. The Tax Reform Act of 1976 set the latter at 5%. A complicated set of regulations governs the calculation of adjusted net income, exclusions for administrative expenses, qualifying distributions to meet the required pay-out. It is important for trustees to be familiar with their general purport and for some foundation manager (trustee, officer, staff or consultant) to understand them in detail and to keep adequate records of income and disbursements.

2. Duty to adhere to charter and donor's wishes. The terms of the trust or founding instrument often set limits, as we have noted, on the performance of the foundation. Some foundations are very general in

6. Most codes of conduct cover staff as well as trustees. Here again full disclosure of any outside connections is the rule. While some foundations permit or indeed encourage staff members to be active in community organizations (San Francisco and Northwest Area, for example), others prohibit such connections (Cleveland and Mott). Outside fees to staff are in general proscribed. The Ford Foundation prohibits acceptance of fees for speaking, consulting, radio and television appearances, but allows directors' fees and authors' royalties. Gifts of more than nominal value may not be accepted. Even honorary degrees must first have the approval of the president. See Frederick Willman: "Are Written Guidelines Useful?" in the May/June 1977 issue of *Foundation News*.

7. The Danforth Foundation had made a practice of building up its capital assets by accumulating part of its income (a practice which many other foundations followed), and it so happened that in the period 1950-52 it was engaged in hiring an executive director and in developing a new program of grants. During this period it continued to spend less than its total income pending new program decisions. The IRS revoked its tax exemption for those years, and this action was upheld in court.

8. The Peterson Commission's Report, *Foundations, Private Giving, and Public Policy*, chapter 9, found in its 1968 survey that 10% of foundations paid out less than 1% of total asset value, 17% less than 2%, 22% less than 3%, and 27% less than 4%.

their charitable purposes; others are restricted in one way or another. It is the legal duty of trustees to carry out the provisions of the charter so far as it is possible or practicable to do so. It is their moral duty to do so by intelligent rather than haphazard grant making, by the development of an overall program, by evaluation of the success of grants made—in short, all the responsibilities discussed in chapters 2, 3, and 4. Some charters establish foundations in perpetuity; others specify that principal as well as income shall be spent within a given number of years; and in yet a third group trustees are left with discretion to spend principal as well as income in accordance with their best judgment.

It is not always possible to carry out the express purposes set forth in the charter, either because they are too narrowly defined or because unanticipated changes in society make "ancient ways uncouth." In this situation trustees may have no alternative but to seek court approval for deviations from specific requirements or through the doctrine of *cy pres* to alter the original purposes, keeping as close as possible to the spirit of the donor's intent. Community foundations frequently accept designated funds with the proviso that the trustees may alter the purposes if circumstances make it necessary.

3. Duty to keep and render clear and accurate accounts. This is part of the law of trusts, the actual requirements varying with different state statutes. The beneficiary of a private trust can demand a full accounting of the trustee, and the courts will enforce his rights. Similarly, named beneficiaries of charitable trusts or the state attorney general acting on behalf of the general public, or some segment thereof, can demand an accounting from a charitable trust or foundation. Federal tax law now requires most private foundations to file annually forms 990-PF and 990-AR which together disclose the financial operations and grant distributions. The Tax Reform Act of 1969 further requires that these forms shall be filed with the appropriate state officer (the attorney general, state tax officer, or other officer charged with overseeing 501(c)(3) organizations) and that the state officer be kept informed of any changes in tax exemption and imposition of taxes. As a consequence state laws are being rewritten to give the attorney general or other officer increased powers of supervision and control. A Uniform Act for Supervision of Trustees for Charitable Purposes has been drafted, though as yet not widely adopted. The chief drawback in state supervision is the lack of adequate funds in the attorney general's office, but the situation is changing. Trustees will find themselves increasingly accountable to state as well as to federal supervision.[9]

Trustees have always been expected to keep clear and accurate accounts of their stewardship, carefully segregated from their personal affairs. The complex requirements of the Tax Reform Act of 1969 makes such accounting doubly important. Full and detailed accounting is essential to safeguard the foundation and its trustees against penalties, and an annual audit by outside auditors is a virtual necessity.[10]

9. Fremont-Smith's article on the "Impact of the Tax Reform Act of 1969 on State Supervision of Charities," referred to in footnote 2, provides an excellent discussion of the problems of federal and state oversight.

10. See Vacin: *op. cit.,* pp. 296-7, for a useful summary of record keeping procedures.

4. Duty to exercise reasonable care and skill in the management of investments is mandatory on all trustees. "The only general rule as to investments which can be laid down is that the trustee is under a duty to make such investments as a prudent man would make of his own property having primarily in view the preservation of the estate and the amount and regularity of the income to be derived.... It involves three elements, namely care and skill and caution. The trustee must exercise a reasonable degree of care in selecting investments. He must exercise a reasonable degree of skill in making the selection. He must, in addition, exercise the caution which a prudent man would exercise where a primary consideration is the preservation of the funds invested."[11] Some states have established by statute a legal list of securities in which trustees of charitable trusts may invest, but in general the prudent man doctrine is the norm. This suggests a reasonable degree of diversity in the portfolio and the avoidance of speculative investments. The latter are prohibited by section 4944 of the Internal Revenue Code with its proscription of any investment which might jeopardize the charitable purposes for which the foundation was established. *A Trustee's Handbook* by Augustus Loring and revised in 1962 by James A. Farr lists the types of investment which trustees would do well to avoid.[12]

An instructive example of the problems and pitfalls is to be found in the case of *Lynch v. John M. Redfield Foundation.*[13] The foundation was created in 1940 for charitable purposes. The three trustees deposited income in a bank which in turn made distribution to various beneficiaries upon authorization by the trustees. In the late 1950s disagreement as to management and grants developed among the trustees. One trustee refused to attend meetings, declined to recognize the other two as trustees, tried to establish a new board without them, filed unsuccessful lawsuits to oust them as trustees, and notified the bank not to honor instructions from the other two. As a result the bank in 1961 declined to issue further payments to beneficiaries without court order or unless all three trustees concurred. Since the trustees could not agree, income piled up in a non-interest bearing account in the bank.

The attorney general brought action in a local court on grounds that the trustees had failed to manage the funds of the foundation in proper fashion by allowing income to lie idle in a non-interest bearing bank account and had failed to carry out the charitable purposes for which the foundation existed. The trial court removed the dissident trustee, but declined to surcharge the trustees for the amount of the lost income. Upon appeal to the higher court, "the court held that the directors of a charitable corporation were held to the same standard as that of a trustee, the prudent man investment rule, and that as a matter of law the directors breached this rule by failing to invest the income during the five-year period. The court further held that good faith on the part of the two directors was no defense where the action was based on

11. Austin W. Scott: *The Law of Trusts*, Little, Brown & Co. 1956, cited by Mulreany, *op. cit.*, p. 1068.

12. Published by Little, Brown & Co. See pp. 199-201.

13. 9 Cal. App. 3d 293, 88 Cal. Rptr. 86 (1970), Schweitzer, P.J.

negligence, and that even though the fault may have rested with one trustee only, all the trustees were liable for the damages caused by the negligent acts of their cotrustee." The appeal court then returned the case to the lower court to determine the exact date of the breach of trust and to surcharge the trustees accordingly.

One of the criticisms of foundations, as noted in an earlier chapter, was their use by wealthy donors to perpetuate family control over closely held family businesses. Section 4943 of the Internal Revenue Code has caused a lot of anguish by its sharp restrictions on anything approaching foundation control of a business, although a schedule for the gradual phase-out of pre-1969 "excess business holdings" was written into the law. In essence, foundations together with disqualified persons may not own more than 20% of the voting stock of a corporation. To this there are two exceptions. If third parties who are not disqualified persons effectively control the business, the foundation plus disqualified persons may own up to 35% of the stock; and second, regardless of the amount of stock owned by disqualified persons, the foundation may own up to 2%.[14]

Section 4945 of the Code prohibits the expenditure of foundation funds for a variety of improper purposes, most of which are discussed in section 6 below. One of the prohibitions is a kind of catch-all in that it sets various penalties against the foundation and its managers for expenditures for non-charitable purposes. Excessive compensation to staff by way of salaries or perquisites, to trustees in the form of honoraria, to consultants and advisers through fees is considered a non-charitable expenditure, though "excessive" is not clearly defined.

5. Duty not to delegate. According to the law of trusts a trustee may not delegate to others actions which he can reasonably be expected to perform. "In essence, this rule states a personal duty on the trustee to administer the trust. His must be the final responsibility and ultimate source of all decisions. He may delegate the performance of administrative tasks to others, may employ counsel, attorneys, accountants, or stock brokers to handle certain matters, and may entrust them with the property of the trust, but he must maintain at all times full responsibility for their acts."[15] Trustees or directors of charitable corporations have somewhat greater freedom to delegate than the trustees of charitable trusts. The law is slowly changing to take account of the need in a complex society for dependence on expert advice, but the fact remains that trustees will in the last analysis be held accountable and cannot plead the delegation of authority in self defense.[16]

---

14. For more details see Vacin: *op. cit.*, pp. 288-9.

15. Fremont-Smith: *op. cit.*, p. 95.

16. Elizabeth E. Baringhaus has made an interesting comparison of English and American law in this respect. See "Trustee's Power to Delegate: A Comparative View" in *Notre Dame Lawyer* for December 1974. She concludes: "The American view of trustees' power to delegate and employ agents is inappropriate in view of the necessities of modern trust administration. The emphasis on an imaginary line which divides ministerial duties from those involving discretion detracts from what should be the central focus: the risk involved weighed against the potential benefit to the trust. The English approach is more sophisticated and more responsive to modern needs. It emphasizes the substance of a trustee's function rather than its form." P. 284. See

A case in point is the recent and much discussed *Stern v. Lucy Webb Hayes National Training School for Deaconesses and Missionaries*, better known as the Sibley Hospital case. The facts in the case are so pertinent to a variety of other situations and Judge Gesell's decision so important that all trustees would do well to familiarize themselves with it.[17] The plaintiffs brought charges of conspiracy, mismanagement, nonmanagement and self-dealing against certain of the trustees of the hospital. Judge Gesell did not find the defendants guilty of the first two charges, but did find them guilty of the last two. The five trustees, who were the chief target of the suit, were all affiliated with one or more financial institutions with which the hospital had maintained significant ties, including low- or non-interest bearing accounts of considerable size. Judge Gesell found them involved in self-dealing and conflict of interest, but declined to assess damages on the grounds that there was no evidence the hospital had suffered from their acts. In his Order he laid down strict rules for full disclosure and for complete accounting of all transactions between the hospital and any of the banks involved.

More important to our present concern was the charge of nonmanagement. The five trustees were all members of the hospital board's investment committee, one was a member of the finance committee and three were members of the executive committee. The hospital's operations were dominated by two trustees, the treasurer and the hospital administrator. For nearly ten years neither investment nor finance committee met, all investments being handled by the strong-willed treasurer and bank deposits by the two dominant trustees. Judge Gesell stated in his Memorandum Opinion: "Trustees are particularly vulnerable to such a charge [failure to supervise the investments and even to attend meetings] because they not only have an affirmative duty to 'maximize the trust income by prudent investment,' but they may not delegate that duty, even to a committee of their fellow trustees. A corporate director, on the other hand, may delegate his investment responsibility to fellow directors, corporate officers, or even outsiders, but he must continue to exercise general supervision over the activities of his delegates.... Applying these standards to the facts in the record, the court finds that each of the defendant trustees has breached his fiduciary duty to supervise the management of Sibley's investments." Finding that the hospital had suffered no material damage from the failure of its trustees, the judge made no surcharges, but specified a number of steps to be taken to prevent a recurrence of the fiduciary breach.

6. Duty to avoid jeopardizing tax exempt status of foundation. This is implicit in all the duties so far discussed, but it may be helpful to

William L. Cary and Craig B. Bright, *The Law and the Lore of Endowment Funds,* 1969, and *The Developing Law of Endowment Funds: "The Law and the Lore" Revisited,* 1974, both published by The Ford Foundation, for excellent studies of the legal problems of delegation and also of investment.

17. 381 F. Supp. 1003 (D.C., 1974). Judge Gesell's Memorandum Opinion and Order, dated July 30, 1974, contain the whole story, which is also summarized in the articles by Myles L. Mace in the *Harvard Business Review* for January/February 1976 to which reference has already been made.

bring some of the dangers out into the open. Proper application must be made for both federal and state tax exemption. Formal notice of such status should be kept on file. Any changes from the original charter must be cleared with appropriate authorities. Annual reports must be filed with various officers, and a variety of other forms and reports duly filed.

In addition section 4945 of the Internal Revenue Code identifies a number of areas as improper foundation concerns. Put in another way, grants in these areas will be classified as "taxable expenditures." The first consists of expenditures to influence legislation. A foundation may support impartial studies on subjects which are under legislative consideration and it may lobby in support of its own vital interests, but the prohibition against lobbying in general is more harsh than the limitations on other 501(c)(3) organizations. The second is grants to aid particular political candidates. Support of voter registration programs is permitted under limited conditions such as complete nonpartisanship and scope of operations not limited to one specific election or to one political area. The third restriction is on certain grants to individuals, such as scholarships, fellowships, prizes and scholarly studies. They are permitted only when based on ground rules approved in advance by the IRS. Finally, grants to other private foundations and to non-501(c)(3) organizations for charitable purposes are "taxable expenditures" unless the granting foundation exercises a high degree of monitoring and follow-up on the use of the grant by the grantee organization. This is known as "expenditure responsibility." It has proved sufficiently complicated to drive many foundations away from grants of this sort, though others are finding that they can manage the supervision and live with the red tape without too great discomfort. Trustees as well as the foundation are liable for penalty taxes in cases of violation, but here as elsewhere written opinion from legal counsel to the effect that a given grant is not a taxable expenditure may relieve the individual trustee from the penalty.

7. Duty to provide sound management. The responsibilities inherent in this obligation have been the subject of preceding chapters. They can be summarized here for the sake of completing the roster of a trustee's legal and moral duties. Trustees are responsible for general policy within the terms of the charter. They must decide on a program for the foundation. They must provide for adequate administration of the program, and that includes making certain that policies are being properly carried out and that grants or internal programs are as effective as possible. They should review and if necessary revise the foundation's goals and methods of achieving them as times and conditions change.

8. Duty to provide a public accounting. The 1969 Tax Reform Act requires the filing of forms 990-PF and 990-AR, and it further requires that the latter shall be made available to the general public. Foundation trustees, however, have a responsibility to go beyond the legal minimum and give a full public account of assets, income, operations and expenditures. This is the subject of the following chapter, and further discussion will be postponed at this point.

This is a formidable set of duties, and it should be clear that no foundation trustee—or any other trustee for that matter—should enter on his trusteeship lightly. There is no longer any place for window dressing on boards. The duties are complex and the penalties significant.[18] The question of liability compensation is difficult. In certain situations the foundation may reimburse a trustee for expenses in defending himself against charges of improper conduct. In others insurance is available either to the foundation or to the individual trustee. But in some situations no protection is possible, and therefore it behooves the trustee to be knowledgeable and alert.[19]

On the other hand, the situation looks worse than it really is. It is important for new trustees to familiarize themselves both with the charter, by-laws and operations of the foundation they are joining and with the general ground rules within which they must act. Like the income tax, the details are complicated, but the main principles are quite clear and understandable. The need for outside professional help—from lawyers and accountants in particular—is greater as a result of the Tax Reform Act of 1969. Certain precautions are in order. But life is full of risks, and the risks involved in serving as a foundation trustee should not deter anyone who enjoys the satisfactions of contributing to the public good.

18. A useful summary of the relevant provisions of the Tax Reform Act of 1969, as amended, is available from the Council on Foundations upon request.

19. Three useful treatments of protection for trustee liability are (with progressive legal complexity): Norman Sugarman, "Penalties on Foundations and Foundation Managers: How to Avoid Them" in the *Proceedings of the Eleventh Biennial Conference on Charitable Foundations*, New York University 1973, pp. 235-57; Donald E. Vacin, *op. cit.*; and Norman A. Sugarman and Robert S. Bromberg, "Indemnification of Officers and Directors of Private Foundations" in *Prentice-Hall, Inc. — Tax-Exempt Organizations*, 1975, pp. 3281-9.

12 Full Disclosure: Public Right—Foundation Need

"Tax exemption is a high privilege. I believe that the operation of a tax exempt foundation is a public trust; and starting from that premise, I believe that all the business, all the transactions, all the receipts, all the investments, all the grants and contributions made by the foundation to individuals and to institutions, are of public concern."

SENATOR CARL T. CURTIS

ACCOUNTABILITY IS A widely, and often vaguely, used current term. Trustees are accountable. But to whom? Under federal and state laws trustees must account to government for their management of the financial operations of foundations, for staying within certain restrictions in grants to other organizations and for fulfilling their fiduciary responsibilities. Because a foundation is affected with the public interest and is in a real sense "a public trust," trustees have a responsibility to give a public accounting of their finances, program, procedures and grants. On both scores—accountability to government and reporting to the public—the foundation record has been poor. On the first, the record, while not perfect, is vastly better than it was. On the second, in spite of steady progress since 1969, the performance of the foundation world is still indefensible.

Let us begin with the legal requirements. In spite of the fact that most foundations are created under various state statutes, most state provisions for registration and supervision have been so inadequate that for a long time there was not even an adequate roster of foundations. This situation is changing under pressure from the 1969 Tax Reform Act. The federal government first required annual reports in 1942, but for a long time returns on form 990-A were so incomplete, inadequate or missing that the IRS lacked the information necessary for supervision.[1]

---

1. See Andrews, *Philanthropic Foundations*, pp. 304-6, and Nielsen, *The Big Foundations*, pp. 295-6, for details on the failure of the foundation world to provide required information.

The Tax Reform Act of 1969, according to Thomas R. Buckman in his Introduction to Edition 5 of *The Foundation Directory*, created a new "information environment." And Alvin D. Lurie, Assistant IRS Commissioner in charge of Employee Plans and Exempt Organizations, reported to the Sixth Annual Meeting of the Southeastern Council of Foundations in November 1975 that his office had noted a dramatic improvement in the accuracy and completeness of foundation returns. Presumably all foundations now file the required forms (990-PF and except for foundations with assets under $5,000, 990-AR or equivalent) both with the IRS and with the appropriate state authorities. National microfilm collections of these forms are available to the public at The Foundation Center in New York and in Washington and the Donors Forum in Chicago. The Foundation Center maintains regional collections in 61 libraries and foundation offices around the country. All but the smallest private foundations are required by law to make form 990-AR available for public inspection at their headquarters for 180 days after it has been filed and to advertise its availability in a newspaper of general circulation.

Even so, in a recent sample of 1,000 returns Andrews found that "fewer than two-thirds of the sampled foundations provided tax returns in which all required schedules were filled out, statistics checked, and some analysis provided."[2] Nor are the reports readily available as required. In May 1974 an enterprising reporter for the *Cleveland Plain Dealer* had great difficulty in examining the 990-AR forms which local foundations had advertised as available. Much argument and return trips were necessary, and in one case he was met by a flat refusal. "Those who operate private foundations," he concluded, "still seem to feel that such institutions should remain private, despite the law."[3]

Nevertheless, it is now true that certain basic information about all private foundations is at long last becoming available to the public. The Foundation Center has done yeoman service in this regard, fulfilling to the extent information is available the mandate of the Gardner Committee to collect and disseminate basic data on all foundations. For the general public, however, or even for those special segments with need for foundation help, this kind of information is not enough. "As a vehicle for meaningful public disclosure, these returns are largely meaningless to the public," write Laurens Williams and Donald V. Moorehead in a technical study for the Filer Commission on tax distinctions between public and private charitable organizations. What is needed are public

2. Richard E. Friedman, "Private Foundation-Government Relationships" in *The Future of Foundations*, p. 185.

3. *Cleveland Plain Dealer* for May 19, 1974. H. Thomas James, president of The Spencer Foundation, in an essay, "Perspectives on Internal Functioning of Foundations" in *The Future of Foundations* refers to an observation of Richard Magat of The Ford Foundation that in May 1971 when most foundations had to file their 990 forms, 981 placed the required newspaper notice in the *New York Law Journal*. Magat's comment was: "However estimable the *New York Law Journal* may be in other respects, its circulation of 8,969 is somewhat less even than the 33,000 lawyers who practice in New York City." And to that James adds: "It is apparent that some foundations will surrender their 'right' to absolute secrecy with the greatest reluctance." P. 212.

reports, widely or selectively distributed, available upon request, outlining the nature of the foundation, its policies, grant programs and restrictions, procedures and finances.

The Peabody Education Fund created in 1867 and the John F. Slater Fund established in 1882, now merged in the Southern Education Foundation, issued annual reports from the beginning. This excellent example was followed by Carnegie, Rockefeller, Commonwealth and Duke. On the other hand, in his study of the 33 foundations with assets over $100 million (in the current *Directory* the number is 38), Nielsen found that "about half the big foundations for most of their existence have not voluntarily reported, and although two-thirds of them were doing so by 1969 this is a relatively recent development."[4]

According to Foundation Center statistics 77 foundations were issuing annual or biennial reports by 1956, and ten years later this figure had increased to 127. The latest compilation by the Council on Foundations (including reports issued 1973-75) lists 463. A breakdown by asset size is revealing:

Assets	No. of Foundations	No. Reporting	Percent
Under $1 million	22,421	66	0.29
$1-$5 million	1,699	137	8.06
$5-$10 million	356	71	19.94
$10-$25 million	265	84	31.7
$25-$100 million	146	73	50.0
$100 million and over	38	32	84.21

It would be unrealistic to expect all the small family foundations to publish annual reports, but this is no excuse for the 2,533 listed in the current edition of *The Foundation Directory.* Indeed, Saul Richman, information officer of the Council, suggests that the 6,000 foundations making grants of $25,000 or more per year "can and should, even if unstaffed, issue at least a simple, inexpensive report."[5]

Community foundations have the best record of making their programs and activities public, and for this there is a very good reason. They need to be visible in their communities in order to attract additional funding. Company-sponsored foundations have probably the worst record, and this provides one more reason why corporations should give serious thought to the proper management of their company foundations. Of the 100 largest foundations of any type in asset size, 36 do not issue public reports; of the 100 largest in annual grants, 33 make no reports. Put in another way, only 17% of the foundations listed in the current edition of *The Foundation Directory* make an effort beyond the minimum required by law to make their programs known to the general public. Of the 6,000 foundations which might do so, 7% issue reports. This

4. *The Big Foundations,* p. 298.

5. "Update on Annual Reports: Coming Out of the Stone Age" in *Foundation News,* November/December 1975, p. 43.

is not a very impressive record, though it is one which is slowly improving.

Nielsen accuses foundation trustees of reflecting an "enclave mentality,"[6] and this is corroborated by nearly everyone who has sought to elicit information from foundations. Zurcher and Dustan had great difficulty in extracting data for their study of *The Foundation Administrator.* When the Minnesota legislature threatened in 1970 to inaugurate a state excise tax on local foundations, it proved extremely difficult for a group of concerned foundation trustees and staff, led by A.A. Heckman of the then Louis W. and Maud Hill Family Foundation (now the Northwest Area Foundation) to rally the other foundations in self-defense and to extract the kind of information necessary for a persuasive case to the legislature.[7] In 1974 The Grantsmanship Center, a nonprofit organization offering information and training programs to organizations seeking funds, wrote to the 5,454 foundations listed in Edition 4 of *The Foundation Directory* requesting information that would be helpful both to the foundations (in avoiding out-of-program requests) and to those seeking help, and making clear that the letter was "not a request for funding, but only for publications for our library." To this letter they received 759 responses (14.5%) of which 532 (10.3%) provided some sort of information.[8]

Why such a passion for privacy? A reluctance to seem to boast about one's good works is becoming modesty, and there are those, like the various Pew Foundations, which have claimed Biblical authority for doing their charity in secret. There are also practical reasons. Reports cost money which might otherwise go to beneficiaries. More public information invites more requests for grants, and since there never is enough to go around, this results in more disappointed people. Public reports unless very detailed, it is alleged, have minimum informational value; and unless very widely distributed are useful only to an "in group" already familiar with the foundation. Superficially plausible, these arguments are not really persuasive, and one suspects that they are for the most part rationalizations of an attitude which, as we have had occasion to note earlier, pervades much of the foundation world. Foundation money is "my money" or "our money." What we do with it, so long as we stay within legally permitted areas, is nobody's business but ours. This is an attitude which extends not only toward petitioners, but also toward government (which has had in the past great difficulty in

6. *Op. cit.,* chapter 16.

7. See Robert W. Bonine, "One Part Science, One Part Art" in *Foundation News* for November/December 1971; and Jeri Engh, "The Minnesota Council on Foundations: Why and How" in *Foundation News* for September/October 1973.

8. The story is told in great, and often amusing, detail in the April-May 1974 issue of *The Grantsmanship Center News.* Sixty-nine replies declined a non-existent grant request. For example: "Your letter appealing for financial support for the Grantsmanship Center was referred to our Contributions Committee for review. The Committee has seriously considered your request and concluded that we would not have any interest in supporting your program at this time. We appreciate your contacting us and providing us an opportunity to review your program. We regret that we must give you an unfavorable reply and wish you the greatest of success with your project."

obtaining satisfactory returns), toward organizations of grant makers such as the Council on Foundations (which only 3% of foundations have joined), and toward each other (though here at long last isolationism is beginning to break down).

That this attitude is wrong has been one of the central theses of this study. As public trusts, foundations have a responsibility to account to the public on their nature and activities. Recognition of this aspect has no doubt been a relatively late development, as Joseph Kiger, director of research for the Cox Committee, suggests in the *Operating Principles of the Larger Foundations.*[9] More recent has been the popular demand for public accountability by all manner of institutions and organizations. If foundations are to be accessible to the general public, or to those sectors of it with which their programs are concerned, they must make themselves known. This is the basis for the recommendations of the members of the Filer Commission and of the Donee Group that all foundations above a certain size be *required* to issue annual reports. And if foundations wish to avoid an inundation of irrelevant requests for funds, a simple way is to make widely known which areas are within their concern and which fall outside.[10]

In addition to these reasons based on principle and convenience is the ultimate clincher: foundations need to be broadly known and understood if they hope to survive. The battering which foundations took in the investigations of the 1950s and 1960s was due in part to a few sins of commission, but far more to many sins of omission. What shocked the foundation community in the 1968 and 1969 hearings in particular was the absence of understanding, on the part of the public and on the part of the Congress, of what foundations were, what they stood for, what they did, how they operated and the social costs of their demise. And for this the foundations themselves have been responsible. If we refuse to divulge information about ourselves, we cannot expect to have friends in time of need. If we maintain a high wall of secrecy around what we do, we invite people to suspect that we have something improper to hide. If we refuse to respond to inquiries, we will make enemies rather than friends. Friedman, in the essay already referred to, suggests that foundations will need to shape up in this matter of public reports or else they can anticipate requirements imposed by legislation, which is precisely what

9. Russell Sage Foundation 1954, p. 105.

10. In an excellent policy statement entitled "Some General Principles and Guidelines for Grant-Making Foundations" issued in 1973, the Council on Foundations says with regard to disclosure: "Out of the public trust vested in foundations grows the need to accept the principle of full disclosure and readiness to share with concerned persons, as well as with public officials, information about objectives and activities. Too often foundations have proved inaccessible and their decision-making processes cloaked in secrecy. Federal and in some cases state legislation now require at least minimal disclosure, but positive steps taken voluntarily to minimize secretiveness can better show the concern of the foundations to serve the public with sensitivity and good faith. A concern for informing the public of what its objectives and activities are—even when very modest—can also often help a foundation's managers gain useful advice and criticism relating to areas of particular interest to them. It also can forestall inappropriate applicants and the irritation of exaggerated expectations let down." *Foundation News* March/April 1973.

the Filer Commission and the Donee Group have proposed.[11] The real danger, however, if foundation trustees persist in going their private way, is not government regulation but government abolition. What is unknown is unimportant. What is not understood is suspect. In their own long term interests more foundations need to tell their story. It is one of which they can be proud.

There are four levels on which foundations can respond. To begin with, they can answer their mail. This is a minimum requirement of courtesy and good relations. Manning Pattillo, former director of The Foundation Center, lists secrecy, the failure to respond to applications and the refusal to see people seeking funds as three of the recurring complaints which came to his attention.[12]

A second level involves the issuance in some form of a public report for public consumption. This can be elaborate and detailed, as are the annual reports of Ford, Rockefeller, Carnegie and other large foundations. It can be a simple brochure or leaflet giving salient facts about assets, grants, areas of involvement, procedures. If necessary it can be a mimeographed sheet or two. But it should be honest, clear, informative and readable.[13] Distribution is a problem and for small foundations an expensive one. Apart from the immediate circle of those involved and those on the periphery, copies could go to local newspapers, radio and TV stations and to public and institutional libraries, and to state and federal legislators. Even if circulation is limited, the fact that information is available to anyone who wants it goes a long way toward removing the curse of secrecy.

Third, the Filer Commission and the Donee Group have recommended that foundations above a certain size hold annual public meetings. "As a corollary of the public information requirement," say the members of the Donee Group, "we recommend that the law require annual public meetings of the governing boards of grantors with $250,000 or more in assets or $100,000 or more in total grants per year. These meetings, which are standard procedures for organizations in other sectors, would include a program assessment; a preview of future priorities; a review of staff and board member selection; a review of major grants; a forum for the public to state grievances and such other matters as members of the public may wish to raise. Appropriate notice to the public and affected constituencies should be required."[14] This is a tall order which has not been met with any detectable burst of enthusiasm from the foundation

11. *The Future of Foundations*, p. 186. *Giving in America*, pp. 164-5. *Private Philanthropy: Vital & Innovative? or Passive & Irrelevant*, pp. 21-3.

12. "Foundation Administration: Standards and Requirements" in *Proceedings of the Tenth Biennial Conference on Charitable Foundations*, New York University 1971.

13. Saul Richman, who monitors the flow of publications from foundations, reports in the article already referred to that the quality of presentation has undergone remarkable improvement in the last few years. His highly useful *Public Information Handbook for Foundations*, Council on Foundations, 1973, has contributed to this improvement.

14. *Op. cit.*, p. 23.

world.[15] It is difficult to see how such meetings would produce any significant results for large national and international foundations with broad purposes and highly diverse constituencies. On the other hand, it might be illuminating and helpful to a community foundation, and, indeed, the Lincoln Foundation in Nebraska has made a practice of opening board meetings to the general public.

Before the idea is discarded out of hand, it would be well to reflect on the experience of The Bush Foundation of Minnesota, one of the 38 top foundations with assets of over $100 million. Under the imaginative and able leadership of former Governor Elmer L. Andersen, chairman, and Humphrey Doermann, executive director, the foundation scheduled an open meeting on the evening of October 5, 1976, in a downtown St. Paul auditorium. Besides public announcements 5,000 invitations were mailed to applicants, other foundations, local community and service organizations, and names on other available lists. Four hundred and fifty people showed up for a half hour of presentation by Doermann of the foundation's program, background, interests, procedures, grant guidelines, followed by an hour of questions and answers. The discussion was lively but courteous. The *Minneapolis Tribune* complimented the foundation in an editorial, suggesting that "similar experiments in openness could benefit other private foundations, too." In summing up the experience former Governor Andersen wrote: "There was no question that it had been informative and helpful to the people who came. It also seems clear that the meeting has enhanced the stature of the Bush Foundation, and thus contributed to a better understanding of all foundations."[16]

Finally, there are the joint actions and the attendant publicity resulting from regional and national associations of foundations. Slowly—ever so slowly at first, but now with increasing momentum— community, state and regional associations are coming into existence. Trustees are discovering the virtues and values of cooperation—the increased effectiveness of joint attacks on problems and of speaking with a common voice.[17]

A fortiori this is true of cooperation at the national level. Trustees seem to have learned little from the investigations of the 1950s, but under Representative Patman's relentless, and at times outrageous, pressure the need for a joint stand began to be recognized. The information collecting work of the Foundation Center took on new significance, and the steady and not always appreciated efforts of the Council on Foundations to tell the foundations' story to the public, to encourage

15. E.g., in a small sample of trustees and staff of Michigan foundations gathered at the Fourth Annual Conference of the Council of Michigan Foundations, February 1976, 66% disagreed with this recommendation, 17% approved, and 17% were undecided.

16. See *Foundation News*, January/February 1977, pp. 6-8, 11, for interpretations of the meeting by the chairman and a member of the audience.

17. See Bertram G. Waters III, "Are Cooperative Associations the Way of the Future?" in *Foundation News* for January/February 1972; and Lawrence I. Kramer, Jr., "Are Regional Foundations the Key to the Future?" in *Foundation News* for July/August 1974. According to the latest count by the Council on Foundations there are 27 regional and local associations.

better foundation performance and to represent the foundation point of view before Congressional committees began to bear fruit. This is not the place or the occasion to sing their praises, but it is pertinent to end a discussion on the need for more and better disclosure by pointing to the Center's and the Council's increasingly important roles in serving all foundations.

13 Summary and Conclusions

"When you die and come to approach the judgment of Almighty God, what do you think He will demand of you? Do you for an instant presume to believe that He will inquire into your petty failures or your trivial virtues? No! He will ask just one question: 'What did you do as a trustee of The Rockefeller Foundation?'"

FREDERICK T. GATES

"As I see it, there is no other way that as few people can raise the quality of the whole American society as far and as fast as can trustees and directors of our voluntary institutions, using the strength they now have in the positions they now hold."

ROBERT K. GREENLEAF

THREE CONVICTIONS—premises if you will—underlie this study of foundation trustees. First, foundations are important to American society. Second, foundations are in danger. Third, the role of trustees is central and crucial.

For most Americans private philanthropy, like motherhood and apple pie, is a natural phenomenon—an integral part of the value system of American society. To a greater extent than in any other country we have sought to cope with our social, economic and political problems by voluntary associations as well as through government programs, and the multiple sources of support, private and public, have been responsible for the strength, diversity and independence of our social experiments. Although foundation grants are only a small fraction—7.5%-8%—of private charitable giving in the United States, foundations play, or are capable of playing, a special and highly significant role. Their stability, continuity, flexibility and freedom from external pressures give them opportunities and influence out of all proportion to their size. However critical one may be of the failure of many foundations to live up to their

97

possibilities, the foundation record is an extraordinary one. Sesame Street, the Green Revolution, penicillin, noncommercial television are a few chapters in the incredible story of what imagination, ingenuity and good will can do for the welfare of mankind.

Why, then, have foundations been the target of so many attacks over the years—the Walsh Commission of 1912-15, the Cox and Reece Committees from 1952 to 1954, the hearings conducted by Wright Patman during the 1960s? On the one side are the conservatives—and probably a majority of foundation trustees themselves belong to this group—who view with suspicion and distrust foundation grants to organizations challenging the accepted order—voter registration programs, civil rights, consumer advocacy. On the other stand arrayed the poor, the powerless, the young, the minorities who are becoming increasingly vocal in their criticisms of the foundations as Establishment institutions. In an address at the annual conference of the Council on Foundations in 1970 Alan Pifer of the Carnegie Corporation put the dilemma succinctly: "Thus, foundations are and will remain on trial before two large and severely polarized sectors of the society—one with deep psychological craving for stability, the other with an equally compelling urge to change. It seems unlikely, as I have suggested, that either group will leave us alone, and the better we defend ourselves against the one the more vulnerable we will be to the other. In this predicament it would seem that we have no alternative but to stake out and occupy some kind of middle ground, narrow as that may become, from which we try desperately to hold fast to our independence."[1]

The danger to foundations consists not merely in being caught between two opposing views of what is best for our society; it comes also from within. As we have seen, foundation trustees are for the most part a self-perpetuating group, a social and economic elite, not particularly eager to seek out better ways of spending the foundation's money, and still convinced that the foundation is their private affair. Not all trustees by any means, but still too many to refute the critics. And since trustees, with far too few exceptions, are the foundation, who they are and how they meet their responsibilities as trustees are crucial questions for the future of foundations.

The major responsibilities of foundation trustees can be subsumed under nine headings.

1. The first and most important is **to recognize that they serve a public trust.** The assets of foundations have been committed to serving the general good, not some private purpose. Trustees are therefore fiduciaries, with the obligation on the one side to respect so far as circumstances allow the terms of the charter or founding instrument and with the obligation on the other to perform faithfully and intelligently as servants of the public. Trustees err in thinking of foundation assets as "our" money, to be expended or given in grants in accordance with their private preferences. What is "ours" is the

---

1. *Foundations on Trial,* published by the Council on Foundations, 1970, pp. 21-2.

responsibility to use the money in our best judgment, subject of course to the terms of the charter, to promote the public interest. Trustees must never forget that they are responsible for "a privately organized public institution."

2. To plan a program or programs of philanthropy. One of the great advantages of a foundation is that it provides an opportunity for systematic giving. Except for the highly disciplined individual, personal giving tends to be haphazard—an expression of strong personal preferences or a response to immediate appeals. This probably characterizes the majority of small family foundations which tend to be an extension of the charitable interests of the donor and his family. The continuity and stability of a foundation, however, make possible the planning of a carefully thought out program. This is particularly important for the large general purpose foundations, but the principle is equally applicable to middle-sized and small foundations.

Every board of trustees should review its program from time to time, re-assess the needs which it might serve or the means by which it could be most effective. This takes time, energy and imagination. It is comfortable to remain in the same old rut. Institutions as well as human beings need re-creation. The responsibility for planning a program of philanthropy carries with it the responsibility for reviewing and revising that program at regular intervals.

3. To make hard choices among public needs. The public good—to enhance which foundations exist—is a very broad concept. Human needs are highly diverse, and the welfare of society is improved by the defense of civil rights, population control and the support of symphony orchestras. How are trustees to choose among these many options?

Some critics, both within and outside government, have accused foundations of being subversive because of their support of controversial issues. Other critics, as noted above, fault foundation trustees for being too conservative. "Controversial" and "conservative" are emotion-laden terms. They reflect the bias of those who use them. For the present the critics on the right can ride comfortably with the restrictions imposed by the Tax Reform Act of 1969. The criticisms most commonly heard come from the other side.

These take two forms. The first accuses trustees of being *conventional.* "I think that most foundations are too cautious in their approach—too prone to concentrate their efforts in areas of the tried and proven," said John D. Rockefeller 3rd, upon retiring from The Rockefeller Foundation board. In spite of the widely heralded myth about foundations as the "risk capital" or the "cutting edge" of social change, their record on the whole is one of caution rather than of innovation. The other accuses trustees of being too *conservative*—of being insensitive to the powerless, the poor and those who hunger and thirst after a different righteousness than their own, and consequently of insisting on their interpretation of public need. There is no simple solution to this dilemma. If we believe in freedom of choice, we must resist all efforts to coerce trustees, whether from the left or from the right. Freedom, however, needs to be continually earned. Its price is not only vigilance, but also sensitivity and breadth of understanding. Foundation trustees are in a favored situation to contribute to the improvement of society, and few would deny that it could stand improvement.

4. To diversify board membership and broaden outlook. Most foundations are, or were at their beginning, donor controlled. This is characteristic of the large number of quite small family foundations and of the company-sponsored foundations, where the parent company provides the funds. Community foundations, the boards or distribution committees of which are appointed by outside officials, community agencies and banks, are a striking exception; and the boards of many middle-sized and large foundations have over the course of time evolved from family members into independent bodies composed of prominent citizens. Others have sought even wider diversification.

There is little disposition to challenge donor or family control of the small family foundations (those with assets under $1 million) which account for 90% of the foundation population and 20% of foundation giving. The filing and accounting requirements of the Tax Reform Act of 1969 may result in many of the small foundations spending themselves out or turning over their assets to community foundations. There is already some evidence of such a trend. There is, however, widespread questioning whether middle-sized and large foundations should continue to operate under family control. The critics argue that the donor and his or her family are less likely to take a broad view of the needs of society and more likely to ride their personal preferences than would an independent board of public spirited citizens. Alongside this argument is the fear of the power of great wealth and the continued control of that wealth—the recurrent American aversion to anything that looks like dynastic control of society. One can argue that, foundations being so small a part of total philanthropy, such a fear is groundless, and that some of the best managed, socially concerned foundations are family controlled. Nevertheless, there remains the widespread conviction that foundations "clothed with the public interest" should be managed by trustees who are independent of family interest.

How to accomplish this is the question. The most vehement critics urge legal requirements that would force all foundations above a certain size to increase over a period of time the number of independent trustees until they become a majority. The mildest advocates would let nature take its course. The inevitable toll on family members and family interest will in their view eliminate in time all family control. In between are those, such as the Filer Commission, who would encourage foundations to give up family control by offering various tax and other advantages for opting for a new, preferred status of "independent foundation."

There is more agreement on the need for diversification of board membership. Such studies as we have of foundation trustees indicate that they are predominantly white, male, Protestant, university educated, well-to-do and in their late fifties or early sixties. A slow change has begun to take place in recent years. The number of women is now 19%. Members of minority groups, while increasing in number, still constitute only 0.3%. More foundation boards are seeking younger trustees. If foundations are to be accessible to a wide range of public needs and voluntary agencies and associations, economic, social and even ethnic diversity among its trustees could be helpful. Foundations should serve the public welfare, as we have seen; but it is also important that they be recognized as prepared to serve the public interest, and the character of the board will be the most persuasive evidence. This does not mean that boards should be composed of "representatives" of various groups. That way lies chaos. A trustee represents only the foundation and its best interests, but his background and experience can provide perspectives on the social scene and the diversity of human needs which will be immensely valuable.

Greater diversity among board members is a step which all foundations can take of their own volition without serious threat to the nature of the foundation. Many of the major foundations have already followed this course. Company-sponsored foundations would do well to enrich their governing boards with non-company community experts. Some family foundations have succeeded in creating considerable diversity in viewpoint by deliberate choice among members of the family. Even the smallest would be strengthened by the addition of one or more independent or "public" members to provide an independent point of view. Whatever one's view of donor control and its future prospects, such additions are one step which trustees can and should take of their own volition.

5. To plan for continuity and renewal of board. In community foundations trustees are normally appointed by outside public officials or independent agencies, but for private foundations the customary practice is self-perpetuation. The first board of trustees is usually selected by the donor. Their successors may be dictated by the trust instrument, by the donor if still active, by family conference or by some one trustee such as the chairman who becomes a dominant influence. Too little thought is given in many foundations to the qualities important for trustees: genuine interest in the affairs of the foundation, broad perspective on society or special knowledge of specific areas, objectivity, a capacity for teamwork. The selection of new trustees is too important to be left to chance; it deserves careful study and is an important responsibility of existing trustees.

Any plan of succession should allow for both continuity and change. Some foundations have definite terms; many make pro forma annual appointments; a few have no provision at all. Common sense suggests that in foundations of any appreciable size, trustees should be appointed for set terms and that these should be staggered so that there is assurance of continuity. Change and renewal are equally important. Institutions like people grow old and need an infusion of fresh ideas. The best way of achieving this is to provide for mandatory retirement upon reaching some given age and setting a mandatory limit on the number of consecutive years of service. Limitation on the length of consecutive service could consist of two five-year terms or three three-year terms or some variation on this formula. This is the most graceful way of bidding farewell to members who have outlived their usefulness, and it is always possible to bring back after a year's absence those members who have proved invaluable. It also makes the choice of a different "type" more palatable, for there is an automatic limitation on the length of service of the new member. Wise planning for foundation boards will include one or both of these provisions.

6. To organize for effective operation. How boards function depends on a number of practical considerations and on the thought given to making the board effective. Without the fund raising chore of most public charities, foundation boards can afford to be small. While Ford, Rockefeller and Carnegie have boards of 17 to 21, most middle-sized and large foundations have 7 to 12 trustees, and the small family foundations even fewer. Serious thought should be given to the frequency, length and place of meetings, all of which will affect the quality of trustee deliberations. One-third of all foundations meet only once a year and another 20% semi-annually. For the larger foundations three or four times a year seems to be the norm, though some meet monthly. Boards which largely ratify the recommendations of staff or of the donor meet briefly; those making major decisions among programs and grants or directing operating programs will need from half a day to two days. Frequency and length often vary inversely, and a case can be made for the advantages of longer and more relaxed discussion at less frequent intervals. Each board must decide for itself how it can function most effectively. An increasing number are discovering that at least one meeting per year in a comfortable setting devoted to reviewing program and directions in some depth can be very helpful.

For the larger foundations some committee structure is a virtual necessity. Some trustees will be better at investment; others, at developing and watching over programs. It saves the time of all the trustees if matters of administration, personnel, budget and finance, investment and audit are assigned to appropriate committees. Except for the smaller foundations and those meeting frequently, an executive committee which can be quickly convened is useful for approving grants between board meetings and dealing with emergencies.

The role of the chairman and in foundations with professional staff the role of the chief staff officer are central to the effective operation of the board. The chairman must lead, direct and set an example to the other trustees. The chairman and the chief staff officer must be able to work closely and effectively together, charting a course subject to board approval, planning the agenda of meetings, helping new trustees to understand the full nature of their responsibilities. The value of board morale is an example of the old adage that nothing succeeds like success. Board meetings should be exciting intellectual experiences and trustees should return home with the satisfying feeling that they have been involved constructively in a valuable activity.

7. To make the foundation accessible. To staff or not to staff is an issue for every foundation board of trustees. The services of professional staff can obviously increase greatly the effectiveness of the foundation, and the more complex the program the more important staff become. The daily business of any organization is time consuming. Letters must be answered, requests for funds investigated, budget and finances carefully watched, official reports filed. Staff should do the leg work, prepare data, see that trustees get the kind of information they need, follow through on grants, assess results. Foundations have been widely criticized for their secretiveness and consequently their lack of accessibility to sectors of the public who have some claim on their attention. Lack of staff has been partly to blame.

All this makes sense for the larger foundations. Staffing is difficult for the smaller ones where the cost of staff would be a disproportionate drain on income. Even here, however, cooperation among foundations would make possible a joint staff member, and it is worth noting that some community foundations are serving a very useful clearinghouse role for small family foundations in their geographical area. Trustees have been slow in recognizing their obligation to be accessible to the public and in seeking out administrative ways to accomplish this. In 1970-71 only 212 foundations had one or more full-time professional staff and 345 had full- or part-time. While staffs have increased by 25%, they remain inadequate.

8. To be familiar with and to fulfill all legal requirements. Some of these have been discussed above—to respect the terms set by the charter, to develop programs which will best realize those terms, to insure efficient administration. Others are consequences of common law, state laws and recent federal legislation, the 1969 Tax Reform Act in particular. The basis on which all else depends is the duty of primary concern for the beneficiaries. As interpreted by the Tax Reform Act, this duty prohibits a wide variety of financial transactions with "disqualified persons" as acts of self-dealing. It is important for all "foundation managers" (the term used in the Act for trustees and officers) to be familiar with the kinds of transactions which are prohibited and to be aware of the range of disqualified persons. It is important also to avoid conflicts of interest, as trustees and frequently staff may have connections with recipient agencies and organizations. A few foundations are developing written guidelines to cover such situations.

The prudent management of assets and the duty not to delegate final responsibility for investments are part of the law of charitable trusts. State statutes and court decisions vary in specifying what actions are permissible and what prohibited, but the general purport is clear. The Tax Reform Act of 1969 laid down additional restrictions on speculative investments and on holdings of business assets which give the foundation or disqualified persons effective control. It also prohibited excessive expenditures in salaries, fees, honoraria and administrative costs.

Trustees have the legal obligation to take such actions as will insure the tax exempt status of the foundation and to refrain from such actions as might jeopardize that status. They must see that required reports are filed, that payout requirements are met, that grants are not made to influence legislation (except for legislation directly affecting the status of foundations), or to aid candidates for political office or to individuals for scholarships and fellowships except through pre-approved programs, or to non-501(c)(3) organizations unless the foundation accepts "expenditure responsibility" for the grants. Various penalties are imposed for violations of these restrictions. Recent court decisions are holding trustees to higher standards of accountability, and it is therefore doubly important that trustees inform themselves of their legal obligations and take great care in meeting them.

9. To give public accounting of activities. Trustees of foundations, with notable exceptions, have been singularly reluctant to publicize their activities. A reluctance to seem to boast about their good works has been one of the deterring factors. A reluctance to be inundated with requests for help has been another. An even more basic reason, however, is to be found in a pervasive attitude, namely that the foundation's business is "our" affair, not anyone else's. So long as the foundation stays within the law, there is no necessity, so it is argued, to justify, defend or expose the foundation's program to the general public.

Unfortunately this is wrong. It follows from the public aspect of foundations that they have a moral obligation to give a public account of themselves. The public has a right to know. As a result of recent legislation, all foundations must now file fairly detailed reports with both the federal and state governments and must furthermore make part of those reports available to any interested party. By collecting and compiling the 990 forms The Foundation Center has taken an enormous step in making available to the interested public the range and character of foundation giving. Most of the largest foundations and a fair number of middle-sized foundations go beyond this and publish annual or biennial reports covering their assets, grants, areas of interest, procedures, personnel, and present or future plans. The latest count lists 463 foundations issuing public reports, and while the number is growing steadily, it is still too small.

Apart from the moral obligation implicit in the legal status of foundations, there is also the factor of self-interest. A major obligation of all trustees is to make sure that the work and contribution to American society of philanthropic foundations are widely known and understood.

This can be done at various levels—by more attention to correspondence where many foundations, particularly smaller ones without staff, are at fault; by publishing annual or periodic reports which can range from the detailed accounts of a Kresge or Northwest Area Foundation to a few mimeographed sheets stapled together; by holding public meetings as both the Filer Commission and the Donee Group have recommended and as a few foundations—e.g., the Lincoln Foundation in Nebraska and The Bush Foundation in Minnesota—have tried; and by supporting joint activities for all foundations through the work of The Foundation Center, the Council on Foundations, and the growing number of regional and community associations of foundations.

*   *   *

Compensation for trustees is a special and slightly troublesome issue. It is the exception rather than the rule, and honoraria, when provided, are for the most part quite modest. It is in the American tradition for trustees and directors of nonprofit organizations to donate their services as a contribution *pro bono publico*. On the other hand, both the time involved and (since the Tax Reform Act of 1969) the risks for foundation trustees have increased. The trustees of private trusts expect fees, as do trust companies when serving as trustees of charitable trusts. If banks receive fees, why not individuals serving as trustees alongside them? There is no simple or single answer. Except where mandated by the trust instrument (and even there the provision could presumably be changed or the compensation declined), each board of trustees must decide the issue in terms of its collective conscience.

Unless trustees are providing special professional services, financial and legal being the most common, unless they are serving as the equivalent of professional staff, there is little justification for high fees. Some of the major foundations provide annual retainers of $4,000, $5,000 or even $10,000, though most pay a fee per meeting ranging from $100 to $500. Trust law permits substantial fees to trustees, and in a few cases foundation trustees have relied on the law to justify fees which most public spirited citizens would consider excessive—fees ranging from $50,000 to $200,000 per individual per year. In view of the strictures against excessive expenditures in the 1969 Tax Reform Act it would be wise to review these and similar fees and to remember that they can easily provide the ammunition for the next round of attacks on foundations.

* * *

It is not enough for foundation trustees to do good. They will be judged by the standard used in the parable of the talents in the New Testament. How well have they done with the resources at their command? Those resources are very considerable. Have they been used as fully and as wisely as they might? "We have in our charge," said Alan Pifer in the address already cited, "a unique social invention for the common good, an institution eminently worth having and worth preserving. We must manage it for the maximum good of mankind in our time and we must make every effort to pass it along to the next generation strengthened from within and reestablished in the confidence of an informed and sympathetic public. That is our responsibility."

It is an enormous responsibility. Like other social inventions, foundations can be discarded if judged to be no longer socially useful or productive. Managed with wisdom, sensitivity and a genuine concern for the common good, their future is bright. The judgment of society will hinge on the performance of trustees.

Sources of Quotations

The sources of the quotations at the beginning of each chapter:

CHAPTER 1

Dwight Macdonald, *The Ford Foundation: The Men and the Millions,* Reynal & Company 1956, p. 3.

Foundations, Private Giving, and Public Policy, The Report of the Peterson Commission, University of Chicago Press, 1970, p. 47.

CHAPTER 2

Alan Pifer, *Foundations at the Service of the Public,* 1968 Annual Report of the Carnegie Corporation of New York.

CHAPTER 3

Orville G. Brim, Jr.: "Do We Know What We Are Doing?" in Heimann (ed.), *The Future of Foundations,* 1973, p. 218.

Frederick deW. Bolman: "The Need to Evaluate a Foundation" in *Foundation News* for January/February 1970, p. 20.

CHAPTER 4

Merrimon Cuninggim, *Private Money and Public Service,* McGraw-Hill Book Company, 1972, p. 253.

CHAPTER 5

Andrew Carnegie, Letter of Gift Establishing the Carnegie Corporation of New York, 1911.

CHAPTER 6

Lewis A. Coser, *Men of Ideas: A Sociologist's View,* The Free Press, 1965, pp. 338-9.

CHAPTER 7

Wilbert E. Moore in *Trusteeship and the Management of Foundations* by Donald R. Young and Wilbert E. Moore, Russell Sage Foundation, 1969, p. 20.

Ambrose Bierce, *The Devil's Dictionary.*

CHAPTER 8

F. Emerson Andrews, *Philanthropic Foundations*, Russell Sage Foundation, 1956, p. 89.

CHAPTER 9

Frances T. Farenthold in a dissenting opinion to the Filer Commission Report, *Giving in America*, 1975, pp. 217-8.

Dean Rusk: "Building a Professional Staff" in *Proceedings of the Second Biennial Conference on Charitable Foundations*, New York University, 1955, pp. 170-1.

CHAPTER 10

Donald R. Young in *Trusteeship and the Management of Foundations* by Donald R. Young and Wilbert E. Moore, Russell Sage Foundation, 1969, p. 41.

CHAPTER 11

Robert H. Mulreany: "Foundation Trustees—Selection, Duties, and Responsibilities" in *UCLA Law Review*, May 1966, p. 1065.

Meinhard v. *Salmon*, 249 N.Y. 458, 164 N.E. 545 (1928), 249 N.Y. at 464, Cardozo, Chief Judge.

CHAPTER 12

Senator Carl T. Curtis in a speech on the Senate floor, December 4, 1969.

CHAPTER 13

Frederick T. Gates to The Rockefeller Foundation Trustees at his last Board Meeting, 1923.

Robert K. Greenleaf, "The Trustee: The Buck Starts Here" in *Foundation News*, July/August 1973.

A Select Bibliography on Philanthropic Foundations

The following are the books, pamphlets and special studies which proved particularly helpful in the preparation of this study. No attempt is made to be exhaustive. Early works are for the most part not listed. References to useful magazine and journal articles can be found in the footnotes. *Foundation News*, published six times a year by the Council on Foundations, deserves special mention for its many excellent articles providing wide coverage and thoughtful treatment of issues vital to foundations and foundation trustees. *The Foundation Directory*, published by The Foundation Center, is the standard reference book on foundations. The Introduction to Edition 5, 1975, by Thomas R. Buckman offers an excellent overview of the foundation field.

Andrews, F. Emerson, *Philanthropic Foundations*, Russell Sage Foundation, 1956. This is a classic study and survey of the foundation world by the dean of all "foundation watchers."

Andrews (Editor), *Foundations: 20 Viewpoints*, Russell Sage Foundation, 1965.

Andrews, *Patman and Foundations: Review and Assessment*, Foundation Library Center, 1968. An interesting summary of the Patman hearings and reports during the 1960s.

Bundy, McGeorge, *Foundation Trustees: Their Moral and Social Responsibilities*, The Ford Foundation, 1975.

Commission on Foundations and Private Philanthropy (the Peterson Commission), *Private Giving and Public Policy*, University of Chicago Press, 1970. A useful survey of the situation at the time of the 1969 Tax Reform Act combined with constructive recommendations for foundations.

Commission on Private Philanthropy and Public Needs (the Filer Commission), *Giving in America*, 1975. The most extensive survey and analysis of American philanthropy in many years, with important recommendations regarding the future of foundations.

Cranston, Alan and Pifer, Alan, *Foundations on Trial*, Council on Foundations, 1970. Two very thoughtful essays, one by a senator, the other by a foundation executive.

Cuninggim, Merrimon, *Private Money and Public Service: The Role of Foundations in American Society*, McGraw-Hill Book Company, 1972. One of the most thoughtful interpretations of foundations in recent years.

Donee Group, *Private Philanthropy: Vital & Innovative? or Passive & Irrelevant?* 1975. A critical appraisal of the report of the Filer Commission by a coalition of public interest, social action and volunteer group representatives.

Fremont-Smith, Marion R., *Foundations and Government: State and Federal Law and Supervision,* Russell Sage Foundation, 1965. Pre-1969, but still a comprehensive and highly useful study.

Giving USA, 1976, Annual Report of the American Association of Fund-Raising Counsel, Inc.

Greenleaf, Robert K., *Trustees as Servants,* Center for Applied Studies, Cambridge, 1974. A short (40 pp.) and thoughtful analysis of the role of trustees. An essay every trustee should read.

Heimann, Fritz R. (Editor), *The Future of Foundations,* Prentice-Hall, 1973. Background papers prepared for the 1972 Arden House Conference of the American Assembly.

Katz, Milton, *The Modern Foundation: Its Dual Character, Public and Private,* Foundation Library Center, 1968. An excellent essay, very much worth reading.

Nielsen, Waldemar A., *The Big Foundations,* Columbia University Press, 1972. A critical and controversial examination of the 33 largest foundations in 1972 by a former Ford Foundation officer who believes that foundations are not sufficiently concerned with contemporary social, economic and political problems.

Pifer, Alan, *The Foundation in the Year 2000,* Foundation Library Center, 1968. An excellent short essay.

Richman, Saul, *Public Information Handbook for Foundations,* Council on Foundations, Inc., 1973.

Struckhoff, Eugene C., *The Handbook for Community Foundations: Their Formation, Development, and Operation,* Council on Foundations, Inc., 1977.

Treasury Department Report on Private Foundations, submitted to the Senate Committee on Finance and the House Committee on Ways and Means, February 2, 1965. Useful factual information, an examination of the major criticisms of foundations, generally sympathetic conclusions.

U.S. Human Resources Corporation, *U.S. Foundations and Minority Group Interests,* 1975. An analysis of the failure of foundations to concern themselves with minority group problems and agencies.

Young, Donald R. and Moore, Wilbert., *Trusteeship and the Management of Foundations,* Russell Sage Foundation, 1969. Essays by two "pros" on the theory and practice of foundation management.

Zurcher, Arnold J., *Management of American Foundations: Administration, Policies and Social Role,* New York University Press, 1972. A useful study of what the title suggests by a former officer of the Alfred P. Sloan Foundation.

Zurcher, Arnold J. and Dustan, Jane, *The Foundation Administrator: A Study of Those Who Manage America's Foundations,* Russell Sage Foundation, 1972. While statistical data are now out of date, this remains the most comprehensive survey of the problems of staffing of foundations.

Four reports by individual foundations on examinations of their role in society leading to new statements of foundation objectives are of particular interest.

The Ford Foundation, *Report of the Study for The Ford Foundation on Policy and Program,* 1949. The famous Gaither Report which set new directions for the foundation.

Helmer, Olaf and Helen, *Future Opportunities for Foundation Support,* 1970, published by the Institute for the Future, Middletown, Conn. Sponsored by the Charles F. Kettering Foundation, the study reports on procedures and conclusions of the effort to review and re-appraise goals for the foundation.

The Rockefeller Foundation, *The Course Ahead,* 1974. A thoughtful statement by the special committee to reassess the foundation's program and directions.

Wieboldt Foundation, *Evaluation Project,* 1973. A readable account of a medium small foundation's review of its program.

The Filer Commission sponsored a considerable number of special studies and research papers, most of which are listed in the printed *Guide to Sponsored Research of the Commission on Private Philanthropy and Public Needs.* The Commission has announced its intention to publish these studies, but as of the present (February 1977) they are available only in duplicated form. They are a mine of information. Some of the most useful to foundation trustees are the following:

Asher, Thomas R., *Public Needs, Public Policy and Philanthropy*

Carey, Sarah C., *Philanthropy and the Powerless*

Council on Foundations, *Revised Report and Recommendations on Private Philanthropic Foundations*

Harris, James F. and Klepper, Anne, *Corporate Philanthropic Public Service Activities*

Mavity, Jane H. and Ylvisaker, Paul N., *The Role of Private Philanthropy in Public Affairs*

Stone, Lawrence M., *The Charitable Foundation: Its Governance*